MILLENNIUM PROPHECIES

Tad Mann was born in New York in August 1943. He received an architecture degree from Cornell University and practised as an architectural designer in New York City and Rome. After a journey to the East he became a professional astrologer in 1972. In 1973 he moved to London, where he raised his daughter, Ptolemy. He now lives in Copenhagen with his astrologer wife Lise-Lotte, teaches astrology and psychology, paints, and is a graphic designer. He is a member of AFAN and SAFA astrological organizations and lectures worldwide.

By the same Author:

The Round Art: The Astrology of Time and Space
Life Time Astrology
The Divine Plot: Astrology and Reincarnation
The Mandala Astrological Tarot
The Future of Astrology
Astrology and the Art of Healing

Millennium Prophecies

Predictions for the Year 2000

by A T Mann

ELEMENT

**Shaftesbury, Dorset ● Rockport, Massachusetts
Brisbane, Queensland**

© A. T. Mann 1992

Published in Great Britain in 1992 by
Element Books Limited
Longmead, Shaftesbury, Dorset

Published in Australia in 1992 by
Element Books Limited for Jacaranda Wiley Limited
33 Park Road, Milton, Brisbane, 4064

Published in the USA in 1992 by
Element, Inc
42 Broadway, Rockport, MA 01966

Cover illustration by Martin Rieser
Cover design by Max Fairbrother
Designed and typeset by A. T. Mann
Printed and bound in Great Britain by Dotesios Ltd,
Trowbridge, Wiltshire

A catalogue record for this book
is available from the British Library

Library of Congress
Cataloguing in Publication Data available

ISBN 1-85230-323-9

For my darling daughter Ptolemy

Acknowledgements

To Michael Mann at Element Books for his support, patience and millennial friendship. To John Baldock for his invaluable reading and comments on the manuscript. To my wife Lise-Lotte for her love and wisdom.

Credits

John Michell for permission to reproduce the illustration from *City of Revelation*, Garnstone Press, 1972.

José Argüelles for permission to reproduce the illustration from *The Mayan Factor*, Bear & Company, 1987.

For permission to use astrological chartwheels from Blue Star Level III and map from AstroMaps computer programs, © 1990 Matrix Software, 315 Marion Avenue, Big Rapids, MI 49307, USA. Tel: 1(800)PLANETS

Contents

List of Illustrations

Table of Millennial Times

Year	Prophet	Prophecy
BC		
5960	The Septuagint	Creation.
4173	Nostradamus	Creation.
4004	Bishop Ussher	Creation.
3952	Josephus	Creation.
3949	Venerable Bede	Creation.
3761	Abraham Judeus	Creation.
3102		Beginning of the Kali Yuga.
2170		Reputed building of the Great Pyramid.
46	Julius Caesar	Introduced Julian calendar.
0		Birth of Jesus Christ.
AD		
33		The Crucifixion
70		Destruction of the Jewish Temple.
156	Montanus	Declared himself an incarnation of the Holy Ghost and prophesied the coming of the Millennium.
365	Early Christians	Believed to be the End of the World.
400	St Augustine	Condemned astrology and prophecy in *City of God*.
525	Dionysius Exiguus	The first use of years AD.
553	Church	Outlawing of concept of reincarnation by the Church.
622	Mohammed	The Hegira and beginning of the Islamic calendar.
794	Charlemagne	Holy Roman Empire established.
1000		The Millennium. End of the Seventh Shemitah, beginning the Jubilee Year.
1033		The Millennium 1000 years after the crucifixion.
1066		Conquest Comet predicted the end of the world.
1496		The Millennium.
1524	Stoffler	The Millennium.
1555	Nostradamus	The first seven *Centuries* published.
1559	Nostradamus	The death of King Henri II.
1583	Bishop Jewel	The Millennium prophesied.
1582	Pope Gregory	Gregorian calendar introduced.
1643	Earl of Essex	Declared himself John the Baptist and predicted the Second Coming of Christ.
1656		The years between Creation and the Flood - a millennium.
1666		The Millennium of the Great Beast.
1681	Bossuet	Proposed using years BC.
1707	French Prophets	The end of the world.
1750	Shora Atahuallpa	The world will be lost in darkness.
1752		England adopted the Gregorian calendar, losing ten days.
1781	William Herschel	Uranus discovered.

Year	Prophet	Prophecy
1792	Napoleon	Egyptian invasion.
1822	Champollion	Decoding of the Rosetta Stone.
1843	William Miller	The end of the world.
1844	Dane Rudhyar	Announcement of the Age of Aquarius.
1846	Le Verrier and Galle	Neptune discovered.
1847	Harriet Livermore	End of the world.
1859	John Taylor	Discovery of the prophecies of the Great Pyramid.
1865	John Menzies	First chronological time scale of the Great Pyramid.
1886	C T Russell	*The Divine Plan of the Ages.*
1889	Nostradamus	Beginning of the Cycle of the Moon.
1895	Alice Bailey	First channelled the Master Koot Hoomi.
1898	Hindus and Buddhists	End of the Kali Yuga.
1904	Aleister Crowley	Beginning of the Aeon of Horus.
1905	Gerald Massey	Beginning of the Age of Aquarius.
1911	Theosophists	Krishnamurti channelled the Lord Maitreya, signalling the beginning of the Age of Aquarius.
1915	Morton Edgar (1924)	Humanity enters on to the Plane of Perfection.
1916	Carl Jung	Vision of the *Seven Sermons to the Dead.*
1919	Alice Bailey	First contact with The Tibetan Djwhal Khul.
1924	Helena Roerich	Transmissions from Master Morya.
1925	Davidson	Decoding of the Great Pyramid prophecies.
1930	Percival Lowell	Pluto discovered.
1931	Alice Bailey	According to Djwhal Khul we entered the Age of Aquarius.
1936	Edgar Cayce	Earth's axis begins to shift.
1943	Edgar Cayce	Atomic, Space or Spiritual Age begins.
1945	Alice Bailey	Final stage of Christ's 300-year mission begins.
1946	Alice Bailey	Receives *The Great Invocation.*
1950	Henry Adams (1903)	The end of the world.
	Catherine Emmerich	The unchaining of Lucifer.
1953	Davidson	An event which will forever alter humanity.
1958	Edgar Cayce (1934)	The beginning of a forty-year period of natural disasters.
1962	Gabriel Jogand (1890)	Birth of the Antichrist.
	Willaru Huayta	Age of Aquarius begins in February.
1965		Uranus/Pluto conjunction in Virgo.
1968	Edgar Cayce	New land will appear in the Caribbean.
	NASA	First man on the moon.
1975	Dane Rudhyar	Avatar of the New Age will appear.
	Alice Bailey	Trans-Himalayan Lodge inaugurates the psycho-scientific ego and Confucius will reincarnate.
1980	Innocent Rissault	The start of the career of the Antichrist.
1980s	Nostradamus	The fall of Communism (IV,32). The Blunt scandal (VIII,87). The papal Bank Ambrosiana scandal (VI,9).
1982	Alice Bailey	In the spiritual hierarchy we are in Solar System II, Earth Chain II, Globe IV, Round IV, Root Race V.

Year	Prophet	Prophecy
1985	Jeanne Dixon (1978)	Comet will strike Earth.
1987	José Argüelles	The Harmonic Convergence.
1989	Ross Peterson (1977)	Earth upheavals until 2030.
1990s	Edgar Cayce	Japan will fall into the sea as a result of volcanic activity. Eruption of Mt Vesuvius and Mt Pelée leading to earthquakes in southern California, Nevada and South America.
	Nostradamus	Third King of the North will appear (Epistle). Coming power of the European Common Market (IV,32; V,51).
1990	Alice Bailey	Teaching of Shamballa will be given out and the Atlantic Charter formulated.
	Nostradamus	US/USSR alliance formed (VI,21; II,89).
	Eliza. Clare Prophet	Cataclysm destroying most of humanity.
1991	Nostradamus	Middle Eastern war involving a man with three water signs (Saddam Hussein) (VIII,70; V,23). The fall of Margaret Thatcher (VI,59; VI,74). Breakdown of USSR (IV,50). Commonwealth of Independent States (V,2; IX,51; VIII,17; VIII,97). Competition between Russian leaders (IX,36). The renaming of St Petersburg and the return of Christianity in Russia (V,78). War in Yugoslavia (IV,82; VI,96).
1992	Max Toth	End of the traditional dating of the Great Pyramid.
1993		Uranus/Neptune conjunct in Capricorn.
	Nostradamus	Russia/US War (IV,95). Islamic unrest in former USSR (III,95). The Third Antichrist 'ALUS' emerges in the Black Sea area of Russia, or from China (V,96; V,54).
1994	Nostradamus	Droughts lasting forty months followed by floods which could initiate a great war (I,16; I,17).
1995	Max Toth	Kingdom of the Spirit arises. Natural and electrical storms plague humanity.
	Nostradamus	French or Spanish papal candidates considered. An unloved Pope elected. Friction from the Albanians.
	Edgar Cayce	Eruption of Mt Taal in 1995 causes catastrophe.
mid 1990s	Nostradamus	Creation of a Palestinian state (III,97). War of Christianity vs. the Antichrist (V,62). Arabian (Islamic) dominance of southern Russia; refugee problems in Europe (VI,80). Antichrist defeats the West and the Russian Commonwealth (VII,59). Water and red hail cover the Earth's surface (VIII,77).
1996	Sun Bear	Three years of worldwide starvation begin.
	Nostradamus	Great heat, burning winds, famines due to ozone layer depletion, environmental catastrophes (IV,67). Destruction of Slavonia (IV,82). Racial differences degenerate intostrife and bloodshed; War between China and Russia (VI,10).
1997	Carl Jung	New Age begins.
	Edgar Cayce (1940)	New York City, Connecticut, South Carolina and Georgia inundated. Great Lakes empty into the Gulf of Mexico.

Year	Prophet	Prophecy
		Second American Revolution from human rights movement.
	Nostradamus	Recapture of Gibraltar (V,35). World War III begins.
1998	Edgar Cayce (1934)	Culmination of forty years of disasters. US coast inundated.
1998	Edgar Cayce (1941)	Japan inundated. Cayce's incarnation as a 'Liberator of the World'.
	Nostradamus	The Antichrist places an antipope on the throne of St Peters; great wars and battles; many deaths leading to a thousand years of peace (Preface). Prince Charles becomes King and extracts his revenge for his brothers (X,26). End of the British monarchy (VIII,97). Raids, great fires and wars caused by meteors; New York City is destroyed by burning sky, widespread fires which cannot be stopped; a king enters the city (V,8; IV,92).
1999	Nostradamus	The Great King of Terror arrives (X,72). Blood and pestilence reddens two rivers (VI,98). Pestilence, famine and natural catastrophes. Armageddon.
	Astrologers	Grand Cross of planets in August.
	Edgar Cayce	Axis shift creates catastrophes.
	Prof. Hideo Itakawa	The end of the world in August.
	Alice Bailey	Consolidation of the forces of evil and materialism on earth. The transition between the Ages of Pisces and Aquarius.
	C. T. Russell (1916)	Time of doom when God's Divine Plan will be revealed.
	7th Day Adventists	The end of the world.
	Criswell (1978)	The end of the world.
	Goodman (1979)	Worldwide earthquakes.
	Fatima (1919)	Worldwide Armageddon.
	Jehovah's Witnesses	End of the world.
2000	Edgar Cayce	Great Alignment of planets in solar system. Major earthquakes in Turkey and Yugoslavia. Sections of the US fall into the sea. Gulf Stream changes course. Parts of British Isles submerge - London on coast. North Sea lands rise. Scandinavia inundated. Hawaii and Japan break away. New climate established. End of the world age, beginning of the New Age. The Second Coming.
	Hebrew scholars	The next Shemitah when Utopian peace will reign.
	Jeanne Dixon (1978)	Geography of earth will be totally altered. Extensive floods.
	Herman Kahn (1974)	Total dominance of the Japanese economy.
	A. Woldben	Age of Aquarius.
	Alice Bailey	Living Christ will resurrect.
2000	Nostradamus	End of the world age. The birth of the Grand Messiah, the Second Coming and the ascent of Christianity. (V,96 and others) The New Arabian Empire will attack Iran, Egypt and Turkey (V,25).
	Innocent Rissault	Final schism of the church and the destruction of Rome. The Antichrist accepted as Universal Monarch.

Year	Prophet	Prophecy
2000	St Malachy	End of the world.
	Garabandal	End of the world.
	Fatima	The Second Coming.
	Margaret Hone	The New Age.
	A T Mann	The Millennium, transition to a new World Age.
2001	Edgar Cayce	Axis shift of the earth will be complete.
	G Barbarin	The Millennium.
2002	Nostradamus	Dreadful war followed by the reign of a new king.
2010	Peter Lemesurier	The Age of Aquarius.
2012	T & D McKenna	Resurrection into the Light of humanity.
	José Argüelles	Baktun of the Transformation of Matter, collapse of global civilization.
2013	Willaru Huayta	End of the Inca calendar.
2020	Adrian Duncan	Age of Aquarius.
2023	A Woldben	Beginning of the Age of Aquarius.
2025	Djwhal Khul	Manifestation of the Fourth Ray. The World Federation of Nations will be formed.
	Max Toth	Final collapse of humanity.
2034	Max Toth	Sign of the Messiah's coming.
2040	Max Toth	The Second Coming, the Messiah is incarnated.
2060	Dane Rudhyar	Age of Aquarius.
2100	Edgar Cayce	Cayce's own future incarnation in Nebraska.
2116	Max Toth	The death of the incarnated Messiah.
2135	Max Toth	Third incarnation of the Messiah.
2160	A Woldben	Beginning of the Age of Aquarius.
	Gordon Strachan	Age of Aquarius.
2250	Nostradamus (1556)	End of the Cycle of the Moon.
2265	Max Toth	Fourth incarnation of the Messiah.
2537	St Vincent	The Millennium.
2813	Robert Hand	Age of Aquarius begins.
2827	Nostradamus	Calculated end of the Jubilee Year.
2874	Morton Edgar	Christ's 'Day of Restitution'.
2915	Morton Edgar	The liberty of the resurrected.
2979	Rutherford	Last date found in the Great Pyramid.
3797	Nostradamus (1555)	End of the world.
6300	Max Toth	The Grand Climacteric.

Frontispiece. The Descent of the Antichrist
(Lucas Cranach, *Nuremberg Chronicle*, 1493.)

Chapter One

The Nature of Prophecy

In the beginning was the Word and the Word was with God and the Word was God.

John, 1:1

As we approach the year AD 2000, it is natural to wonder what will happen to us and our planet Earth. Will we see a planetary catastrophe, Armageddon, the Last Judgment, or will we enter the Age of Aquarius? Will Christ come again? Is this the end of the 360,000 year Kali Yuga, the 'Age of Misery' described by Indian sages? Will the Earth's axis shift, fracturing half of California into the Pacific Ocean?

Nostradamus, Edgar Cayce, the Seventh Day Adventists and many others prophesied the End of the World in the year AD 2000. For many Christians, it will be the Second Coming of Jesus Christ. It is clear that the current problems of overpopulation, famine, political instability, the nuclear threat, pollution, AIDS, the holes in the ozone layer, and the collapse of international banking, economic and governmental institutions are getting worse. They may be even greater problems in the year 2000 than they are now.

The subject of this book is what prophets throughout history have said about the Millennium. There is a remarkable agreement in prophecies dating back to the Biblical books of *Daniel* and *Ezekiel*, the New Testament book of *Revelation*, Christian saints and mystics, the magi-cal *Centuries* of Nostradamus, the visions of Edgar Cayce, medieval crackpots and modern eschatologists, and the astrologers. It is as though some of them could see into the future. *Millennium Prophecies* will present the historical context of a range of prophecies about what will happen at the end of the Millennium.

You will see whether there is agreement about what changes will occur, and when they will happen. The ultimate choice about which prophecies are correct will be left up to you. And when you have seen the evidence, you can decide whether to prepare for Armageddon or for the thousand years of Peace of the Aquarian Age.

Time and Human Nature

> What concerns us here is not calculable time. Rather it is time's abrogation and dissolution in the alternation of tradition and prophecy, which lends to the phrase 'once upon a time' its double sense of past and future, and therewith its burden of potential present.[1]

In early times, it was essential for survival to know when the winter cold would come, when fruits and berries would ripen, when animals would migrate and when the spring thaws would come. The regular seasons and the cycles of nature were an integral part of tribal knowledge, but human behaviour remained unpredictable.

The desire to foresee what will happen tomorrow, next week, or next month is a distinctly human characteristic. Animals live immersed in time, while we must learn about time. A critical aspect of our early upbringing is learning about time and its passage, and understanding how to deal with and organize our time. We are taught to 'think ahead' and 'plan for tomorrow', and our success in life can depend upon these axioms.

We also project our experience from the past into the future, and in a way wager that our vision of the future will correspond to reality. We crave knowledge of what will happen in our emotional and working lives. If we had the knowledge that a present course of action will be successful this would justify current strategies. To know that a present course will be unsuccessful would require that current directions be modified. The future looms ahead of us, containing both the potential for greater security but also the fear of eventual death. In recent times our personal future has become tied up with the survival of the entire planet, making projections infinitely more complex. We need even more urgently to know more about the future.

Understanding the Future

Humanity has developed a number of ways for attempting to deal with the future: planning, prediction, divination and prophecy.

We *plan* by projecting current patterns into the future. We know when we will be paid each month, when our annual holiday is due, when our children will leave school and when we will retire because these are either pre-determined or planned by us. We attempt to impose our will on to our future as much as possible to lessen the sense of the randomness and unpredictability of life. Some people are able to have the vision and strength to control their future, but planning is always affected by incidents or larger trends which can disrupt it and few aspects of our lives can be accurately planned ahead, especially in these uncertain times.

We *predict* or foretell what will happen by extrapolating information that we know. Bookies determine the odds for betting based on past performances and the current popularity of horses to the punters. Economists base their predictions on past trends and economic cycles they have observed in the past. Prediction is all around us. We see analysts on the media projecting economic cycles which will determine how much our salary, property or investments will be worth, weather patterns which will affect our weekend or holidays, population patterns showing how crowded our planet will become. The insurance we are forced to take out is carefully weighted in favour of the insurance companies. Odds are quoted on this afternoon's races, the likely numbers in the lottery and the weekend's football matches, and endless calculations show our impending doom from the increase of pollution in our atmosphere and on our Earth, and the progressive disappearance of the protective ozone layer. Predictions are informed projections. It would be true to say that the prediction of the future affects most areas of our life.

Divination means 'from the divine', and is the process of arriving at the answer to a question by interpreting patterns created by nature or artifice, such as birds in the sky, the entrails of sacrificial animals, thrown bones or stones covered with strange images, the division of yarrow stalks or the laying of tarot cards. The diviner ceremonially casts the oracle or meditates on some aspect of his environment, interprets its significance and projects its meaning into either past, present or future. The diviner is a *conscious* interpreter of divinatory images or information, and is guided by an understanding of patterns.

Prophecy means 'to speak by divine inspiration', and a prophet is someone who speaks forth about a received revelation. Prophecy is a gift from God or the gods, a transmission from the intelligence of the universe. Prophecy happens spontaneously, and prophets are often unaware of the implications of their transmission. Prophetic pronouncements are much like dreams in that they are often difficult to order in time, or to decipher. Some of the most important prophets were unable to interpret their own prophecies.

A critical difference between divination and prophecy is that divination is directed towards determining the answer to a question or the significance of a particular action, whereas prophecy is not necessarily directed toward any particular objective. Prophets are often unwilling or resistant to their role, while the diviner acts from choice.

Despite their fundamental differences, the circumstances of divination and prophecy are sometimes similar. Both involve tapping into the unconscious mind, whether voluntarily or involuntarily. Monks, magicians, mediums and meditators all invoke prophetic powers by sitting in a relaxed state and opening themselves up as a channel for what will or will not pass through them. The transmission may be inspired by sacred music, drumming, repetitious mantras, incense, hallucinogenic drugs or chemicals, sympathetic places, symbolic imagery or a host of other aids or devices. The modern American clairvoyant Edgar Cayce[2] (1877-1945) was able to enter a trance on demand simply by lying down in his office. Most prophets do not have such control over their channel, and are forced to wait for contact with the disembodied master.

The information received by prophets varies dramatically in clarity, form and content. Sometimes a prophecy is received as a dream with unusual juxtapositions of vividly contrasting or paradoxical images, such as St John's horned demons and beatific spirits. In such instances, a verbal description of the description of the prophecy may be hopelessly inadequate.

The prophecies of the famous French prophet and astrologer Nostradamus[3] were received as images and converted into four-line quatrains. Nostradamus stated that to avoid persecution he consciously jumbled the sequence and obscured the clarity of his received images. He used a strange combination of ancient and modern languages, astrological and alchemical symbolism, and abstruse allusions in the quatrains. Like the utterances of the priestesses of the Delphic Oracle in ancient Greece, prophecies can be interpreted in a number of ways that are frequently contradictory.

Deciphering prophecies is like interpreting dreams. The time sense is often confused, the imagery may be personal to the dreamer (or prophet), and the true meaning can be as unknown as the source of the transmission. Do they come from God or from the unconscious of the prophet? It is often difficult, if not impossible, to tell. The great depth psychologist Carl Jung defined the existence of the *collective unconscious*, the layer of the unconscious which lies beneath the personal unconscious and which is common to all humanity. In a sense it is the legacy of our common past, stored within us, awaiting discovery. Jung found a similarity of imagery in individual dreams and the myths of many cultures, including those of early civilizations. Under the veneer of civilization lies a potent world of images of angels and demons. If we resist expressing this world within us, it breaks through into consciousness when we least expect it. Exposure to prophecy has had a magical and evocative effect on our awareness for thousands of years, probably because of this link with the unconscious. The power of prophecy is great because it taps into the collective unconscious and resonates with us, all of us.

Prophets speak for us because they receive information from the collective unconscious and uniquely are able to describe or express such wonders to those who cannot or do not wish to receive it.

Prophecy and Astrology

The relationship of astrology to prophecy is complex and contradictory. Many of the most famous prophets were also astrologers, such as Nostradamus and the biblical prophet Ezekiel. Astrology is a science which utilizes the intuitive faculty in interpretation. This intuitive factor is what some call the 'art' of astrology, as distinct from its rational mathematical foundation. Nostradamus claimed to be a prophet who utilized the language of astrology to determine the timing and sometimes the protagonists in his prophecies. He blended the two disciplines in his own inimitable way, which may explain the power it has had over many successive generations of commentators and the public.

Astrology is a useful language for prophets because of its system of correspondences. For example, the planet Mars corresponds to change; the colour red; the male sexual principle; fever; energy; aggression, fights and battles; the adrenal gland which produces the human 'fight and flight' mechanism; the metal iron; the ruby and other red stones or minerals; the homoeopathic remedy Aconite; and many other qualities and substances. If the planetary energy of Mars is activated in a horoscope, it will manifest itself by utilizing a range of martial qualities as a way of activating the 'Mars' energy within the individual. It was believed that when the red planet was prominent in the sky, it incited individuals and nations to fight each other.

In describing his prophecies, Nostradamus correlated the signs and planets to places, nations, cities, types of people, specific individuals and the qualities and events associated with them. This produced a breadth and depth to his prophetic quatrains which allowed subsequent interpreters to apply them in a number of ways. It is difficult to know whether Nostradamus had only one specific event in mind for each quatrain. In an *Epistle* to his son Caesar he implied that he did, but the evidence of the prophecies and their application to subsequent historical events shows that they may be applied to many events. This has brought a more universal relevance to his work and also protected him from prosecution during his own time. The inquisitors were always seeking to prosecute him for the slightest mistake.

Intuitive Prophets

Many of the shapers of world thought were intuitive, and the most illuminating mathematicians and scientists utilized their intuitive faculty. Great breakthroughs in experimental science have often come through dreams or fantasies. In some sense they are prophecies as well. The idea of the benzene ring came to the German chemist Kekulé through a vision of a circle of figures holding hands.

I turned the chair to the fireplace and sank into half-sleep. The atoms flitted before my eyes. Long rows variously, closely unite; all in movement; wriggling and turning like snakes. And see, what was that? One of the snakes seized its own tail and the image whirled scornfully before my eyes. As though from a flash of lightning I awoke . . . Let us learn to dream, gentlemen.[4]

Descartes discovered what he thought was the key to rational science through a vision.

Einstein's Theory of Relativity came through a vision he had while travelling to work on a tram in Basel in his early twenties, and it subsequently took a decade to describe and prove it.

There is no logical way to the discovery of these elemental laws. There is only the way of intuition, which is helped by a feeling for the order lying behind appearance.[5]

Should we attribute these important discoveries to the scientific method or prophecy? It is unfortunate that in our society the very word prophecy is associated with the irrational, the mentally deranged and the fantastic. On the contrary, one of the greatest scientists has stated:

What I prophesied twenty-two years ago . . . at length I have brought to light, and have recognized its truth beyond my most sanguine expectations.

So said Isaac Newton about the discovery of his third law.

Our society is built on the observation of repetitive phenomena which recur as we anticipate them, and we tend to exclude from our 'logic' those phenomena which are not repetitive, or whose cycles are difficult to ascertain. We prize and use electricity even though we cannot understand what it is, because it is predictable. Prophecy is unacceptable until the prophet has been proven accurate. Fact and prediction may organize our lives, but prophecy opens up the mystery and essence of life.

The Millennium

As recently as the late sixteenth century it was believed that Creation was an event at the beginning of historical time. Based upon the genealogies of the Bible, Nostradamus reckoned that the time from Creation to the Great Flood was 2106 years, based on the lifespan and time periods given in the biblical book of *Genesis*. Thus he could state that he lived exactly 4173 years and eight months after the Creation.

Scholars debated the number of years which had elapsed since Creation. The Bishop Ussher dated Creation to the minute. This seems absurd, knowing as we do the impossibility of such a recent and 'real' time for Creation, but to the ancient, medieval and even Renaissance mind it was natural.

Given such apparent precision in dating Creation, it was deemed possible to predict historical events and even people's lives if the key were known. This allowed a minimal freedom of will, but it was accepted with resignation that God determined the inexorable march of time into the future, just as the Old and New Testaments described its precise past.

This ancient view of history contained an important idea — the cyclical nature of time. Finite history had a discrete beginning, and also an end. The Bible begins with the Creation in *Genesis* and ends in the cataclysm of the book of *Revelation*. The belief that the world has a definite duration and is tending toward its end is the concept of the 'Millennium'. While the term literally means one thousand years, it has also come to mean the end of the world age, the end of the world, or the Last Judgment.

Millennial cultures believe that history is a ritual process, a repetitive recreation of a sequence of events which culminates in the end of the world. In such societies this ritual sequence is reiterated in daily, seasonal, yearly and generational rituals.

Rituals, the outer forms of myths, were based on appeasing the gods and were related to, and often derived from, planetary movements or seasonal phenomena. Acts of worship repeated these archetypal actions in historical time. Primitive humanity identified with gods and the cosmos, an integration missing in our modern 'scientific' world. Mythic histories postulated the periodic regeneration of the world, times of respite and rest. This concept lies at the heart of the major world religions, including early Christianity. The Millennium has an additional meaning as the time of Universal Salvation.

Just as humanity inherited primordial sin in the Garden of Eden, so at the end of the world the souls of the just will return, achieve salvation and, led by Christ, will be reborn. The Christ is the 'cosmic man' who enacts the historical process within his own being, just as we can experience His being within us and, by extension, experience universal unity with God. Christ is a symbol of the process of death and rebirth, expressed in his own life and being.

The Nature and Measurement of Time

The concept of time as an objective phenomenon is relatively recent. Early humans lived embedded in a timeless natural world. Each day the Sun rose and travelled across the sky to disappear at sunset. The Sun was worshipped as the bringer of light because if the Sun failed to rise, they knew life could not continue. It sounds silly to us, but was terrifying to them. They could not comprehend that planetary movements were mechanical. Instead they believed that the Sun was a wilful god that required sacrifice and worship, otherwise he would leave their lives in darkness.

Similarly, the Moon crossing the night sky evoked wonder and fear, particularly because she, despite being so prominent throughout the month, disappeared for three days during her cycle. The reappearance of her slim crescent evoked a collective sigh of relief as the Goddess returned to bless the night skies. To this day the Islamic calendar month begins with the first reappearance of the crescent Moon.

The development of astrology in Babylonia, Chaldea and Egypt provided a more accurate means of predicting the future. They projected astronomical tables far ahead, and control over this information provided the priests with powerful leverage over their kings and society at large.

The worship of the sun god Ra was central to the highly sophisticated Egyptian religion. The barque (boat) of the sun crossed the sky each day as the stars and moon crossed the night sky, personified as the sky goddess Nut. Nut's body *was* the night sky,

Figure 1. Joseph Interpreting the Pharaoh's Dream
(Schedel, *Nuremberg Chronicle*, 1493.)

across which the heavenly bodies travelled. Because of the similarities perceived between night and death, Nut was shown inside coffins and vaulted Egyptian tombs.

Myths associated with celestial gods and goddesses persisted well past the Renaissance five hundred years ago, if only in folk tales, fairy tales, verbal mythologies and figures of speech. Astrology still carries mythological associations with the gods and goddesses through the names of the planets, and its popularity shows how powerful the celestial deities still are within us.

In modern depth psychology and psychotherapy the presence of the gods and goddesses within is acknowledged in books such as *The Goddesses in Everywoman* and *The Gods in Everyman*, by Jean Shinoda Bolin, although it is clear that both women and men contain archetypes of both goddesses and gods. However, one key to understanding mythology lies in the mysteries of the larger cycles of time.

Chapter Two

Zodiacal Mysteries

The Great Year

To early astrologers, the cyclic nature of the individual planets naturally led to the assumption that life on Earth was governed by longer cycles of all the planets. The Great Year (*Annus Magnus*) was conceived as being the period of time it would take for all the planets to return to their places at Creation. It was understood that time had a beginning and an end, and that history would end and repeat itself again in exactly the same sequence. Many differing lengths were proposed for the Great Year, but it was agreed that history had a definite duration.

We question such a concept because of the discovery of the three outer planets Uranus, Neptune and Pluto in the last two centuries. Before the discovery of Uranus in 1789, Saturn was the known planet farthest from the Sun. As the cycle of Saturn's revolution around the Sun is only $29\frac{1}{2}$ years, it seemed logical that the great cycle of all the planets was repeated periodically, although ancient astrologers did not know how to determine its duration.

It was believed that there must have been a particularly significant astrological configuration involving all the planets in the remote past which would occur again. It followed that the events determined by such a configuration would also recur. Since the configuration would have been preceded by the same astrological cycles, it was believed that history recurred again and again in the same sequence.

This view of history, called 'eternal recurrence', was prevalent in the ancient world, and accepted by great philosophers such as Plato and Pythagoras and the German Frederich Nietzsche. The Stoic philosophers Zeno and Chrysippus believed that identical world ages repeated down to the smallest detail, and that all humans relived their lives again. This belief gave rise to the word 'stoicism', which means blind acceptance, passionlessness, or indifference to life.

A popular theory was that all planets started at 0° of the first zodiac sign Aries and that when they returned to that position a world age would end. It was assumed that world ages repeated identically in sequence, in an eternal recurrence.

Some calculations of the length of the Great Year were as follows:

I Hsing (Eighth Century)	96,961,740 years
Mandaeans	480,000 years
Lindos astronomer of Rhodes	290,000 years
Wu Lin-Chuaun (Thirteenth Century)	129,000 years
Origen and Hipparchus	36,000 years
Siger of Brabant	36,000 years
Hericlitus	10,800 years
Aristarchus of Samos	2484 years

In the Christian tradition the death and rebirth of the world was described by exact dates. Since the Bible contained the lifetimes of the early prophets and stated the periods of time which had elapsed since Creation, scholars attempted to determine the age of the world and the planetary positions at Creation, reasoning that a return to that position would signal the end of a the world age.

The world was also seen to parallel the life of Christ. Indeed, the mystery of the resurrection applied both to Christ and to the world. The Christian sacraments were re-enactments each day of the series of important events in the life of Christ.

The age of the world was an intensely debated subject, with a range of interpretations, all argued in scholarly ways and with persuasive logic. The Great Year was a central theme of most early Christian histories. The Septuagint dated Creation at 5960 BC, Josephus at 3952 BC, the Venerable Bede at 3949 BC, Abraham Judaeus at 3761 BC, and the Bishop Ussher at six o'clock in the evening of 22 October 4004 BC!

The following quote from the 'Epistle to Henry II' in the *Centuries* shows the logic of Nostradamus on this matter:

For the stretch of time of our forefathers [i.e. the age of the world] which has gone before is such, submitting myself to the direction of the soundest chronologists, that the first man Adam, was about one thousand two hundred and forty years before Noah, computing time by taking simply the Sacred Scriptures for the guide in my astronomic reckonings, to the best of my feeble understanding. After Noah, from him and the universal deluge, about one thousand and fourscore years, came Abraham, who was a sovereign astrologer according to some; he first invented the Chaldean alphabet. Then came Moses, about five hundred and fifteen or sixteen years later. Between the time of David and Moses five hundred and seventy years elapsed. Then after the time of David and the time of our Saviour and Redeemer, Jesus Christ, born of a pure Virgin, there elapsed (according to some chrono-graphers) one thousand three hundred and fifty years.[1]

Based on this information, Nostradamus dated Creation about 4,000 years before Christ. This was particularly important because the dating of his prophecies was based upon it.

The Precession of the Equinoxes

While the length of the Great Year was based on spurious planetary cycles, the phenomenon of the 'precession of the equinoxes' was an astronomical phenomenon discovered by the Egyptians. (Figure 2.)

The angular inclination of the Earth's axis creates the seasons — the northern hemisphere points towards the Sun for half of the year and away from it the other half. As the Earth rotates around its axis in an imperfect cone shape, its axis pointer (the North Pole) describes a very gradual backward circle. This axis makes a complete rotation in about 25,000 years. This backwards movement through the zodiac signs is responsible for the zodiacal ages. The dawning of the Age of Aquarius follows the polar axis leaving the sign Pisces, where it has been for the last two thousand or so years.

Jesus Christ is associated with the sign Pisces, the Fishes. During the Age of Aries from 2000 BC until the time of Christ, ram cults developed in the middle east and elsewhere. The Age of Taurus, from 4000 BC to 2000 BC, had bull cults such as those of the Egyptian Apis.

The astronomical precessional cycle is now known to be 25,725 years, but it is unclear exactly where the constellations begin and end, so the exact dating of the Age of Aquarius has been the subject of

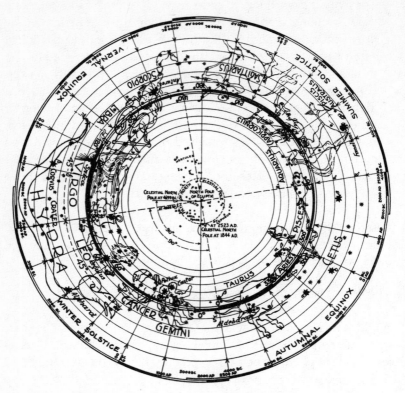

Figure 2. The Precession of the Equinoxes

A plan of the Celestial Hemisphere north of the ecliptic. The outer scale of years gives the dates precession of the Equinoxes and Solstices through the Zodiacal signs. In the almost six thousand years since 4699 BC, the precessional point has moved about 90° in a counter-clockwise direction. (From *The Great Pyramid* by D. Davidson and H. Aldersmith.)

intense speculation and debate (see Chapter Ten: Dates for the Beginning of the Age of Aquarius, on p. 115). Many believe that the entrance of the zodiacal pointer into Aquarius will herald a time of brotherhood and peace, with the focus shifting from the devotional religion of Christianity to a 'New Age' based on a synthesis of universal religious principles.

The precessional world ages have created a phenomenon which has affected the course of history — the concept of the Millennium.

Chapter Three

The Millennium

The history of prophecy stretches back into our collective past. Many of the major world religions originated with prophetic contacts — Moses received the *Ten Commandments*; the Buddha's enlightenment while meditating under the Bodhi tree; the transmission of the *Gospels* to Jesus' disciples in visions; St John and his *Revelation*; Mohammed's reception of the *Koran* from the Archangel Gabriel; Joseph Smith's transcription of the *Book of Mormon* from golden plates to which he was divinely directed in Palmyra, New York; and others. These prophetic transmissions have determined humanity's beliefs, and continue to do so to this day.

An Ancient Egyptian Prophecy

The *Papyrus Anana*[1] was written by the Chief Scribe and companion to the Pharaoh Jentle Leti II in about 1320 BC and provides a fascinating insight into the prophecy of ancient times — it implies a Millennium to come.

Behold it is written in this roll. Read ye who shall find it in the days unborn, if your gods have given you the skill.

Read, O children, of the future and learn the secrets of the past which to you is so far away, and yet truth is so near.

Men do not live once only to depart hence forever, they live many times in many places, though not only in this world.

That between each life is a Veil of Darkness. The doors will be open at last and show us all the chambers through which our feet wandered from the beginning.

Our religion teaches us that we live on eternally . . . now eternity, having no end, can have no beginning; it is a circle. Therefore, if one be true, namely that we live on forever, it would seem that the other must be true also . . . namely, that we have always lived.

To men's eyes God has many faces and each swears that the one he sees is the only true God, yet they are all wrong, for all are true.

Our Kas, which are our spiritual selves, show themselves to us in various ways. Drawing from the infinite veil of wisdom, hidden in the being of every man, they give us who are instructed glimpses of truth and the power to work miracles.

Among the Egyptians, the scarabæus beetle is no god, but a symbol of the Creator, because it rolls a ball of mud between its feet, and nests therein its eggs to hatch; just as the Creator rolls the world around, which seems to be causing it to produce Life.

All gods send their gift of love upon this Earth, without which it would cease to be. My faith teaches me more clearly, perhaps, than yours, that life does not end with death, and therefore that love being life's soul, must endure for eternity.

The strength of the invisible time will bind souls together long after the world is dead. In the end, however, all the various pasts will reveal themselves.

The ancient circular view of time and all that it implied led to the belief in reincarnation which was the central concept in Egyptian and other religions. And a circular view of history postulates a Millennium when all souls will be raised again. *Millennium* means 'a term of one thousand years', but as already mentioned, has come to mean the time of the second coming of Christ, the end of the world age, or the transition time to a new zodiacal precessional age.

Biblical Prophecies

> Then the moon shall be confounded and the sun ashamed, for the Lord of hosts shall reign . . .
>
> *Isaiah*, 24:23

The Hebrew sacred teachings were derived from the prophecies of Moses, contained in the five books of the Pentateuch. The major prophets to follow him were Joshua, Isaiah, Jeremiah, Ezekiel and

Daniel. Indeed there were so many books attributed to them and a multitude of minor prophets that the rabbis had difficulty identifying which books should or should not be included in the Old Testament of the Bible.

The Jews were characterized in the ancient world by their unique attitude to history. They were the first monotheists — there was one God, and the Jews were His 'Chosen People'. Jehovah controlled time and history and his worship created fantastic expectations in the face of the extreme hardships the Jews have faced for thousands of years to this day.

The central concept of Jewish apocalyptic literature is that, following a great catastrophe, there will arise a Palestine which will be a new Garden of Eden, a Paradise on Earth. It was believed that before the attainment of Paradise there would be a Final Judgment. Israel's enemies would pay for their persecution of the Chosen Ones, and righteousness would prevail. All difficulties were therefore considered the direct result of the Jewish people letting their God down in some critical way, either through impious worship or ungodly behaviour. Jehovah was a wrathful, severe and uncompromising patriarchal God.

The tradition of Jewish prophets can be symbolized by the second century BC book of *Daniel*. After centuries of peace, the Jews came under Seleucid control and disagreed about whether their community should adopt Greek customs or maintain the simple behaviour and beliefs of their ancestors. The dream of Daniel is similar to the vision of Ezekiel in that he saw four beasts symbolizing the four fixed signs of the zodiac — Taurus, Leo, Scorpio and Aquarius — amidst the powerful world forces acting upon them. The Greek demon devoured the whole Earth and broke it into pieces, only to be overcome by Israel in the form of the 'Son of Man'. Due to acts of valour and bravery, Israel was not only given Jerusalem, but the entire world as a reward.

The motif of an evil world dominated by tyrannical powers of endless demonic, destructive potential until Jehovah would rise up and overcome the dark forces is a powerful archetypal image. It is also a propaganda tool which the Jews have utilized for millennia and have passed on intact to the Christian world.[2] Their wish for a Saviour to lead them from humiliation is characteristic of the religion. As their political fortunes declined and they were indeed persecuted by the Romans, the powers anticipated of the Saviour became superhuman.

The Messiah in the prophecy of *Ezra* is the Lion of Judah who banishes the Roman eagle, which bursts into flames and is consumed. The Jews became more and more fanatical and suicidal in their expectations, leading up to the destruction of the Temple in AD 70.

After the time of Jesus Christ, the Jewish millennial prophecies were inherited by Christianity, and indeed became the very core of Christian doctrine. The Christians believed that Christ would return and justify the persecutions of the early Christians in His Name. In the prophecy of *Matthew*, the Son of Man will return and reward all men according to their works. The redeemed world to come, when the wrongs of history could be righted, was eagerly awaited and influenced the entire focus of Christianity.

The Christians believed Jesus would return and establish a kingdom on Earth which would remain victorious for thousands of years. The expectation of this millennium of peace and prosperity contrasted with the violent realities which they experienced, especially after the Fall of Rome and the invasion of the Empire by barbarian hordes.

It is a central quality of early Jewish religion that reality is 'veiled' so as not to be known by the profane. The book of *Enoch* describes a cosmic curtain which contains the images of all things which have been brought into being since the day of creation. Everything has its pre-existent reality in the heavenly spheres, and all people, their generations, the events of their lives and their actions, are all part of the fabric of this veil. All actions lead ultimately to the final struggle between good and evil culminating in the appearance of the Messiah at the Millennium.

The dating of history by Jewish scholars was focused toward discovering the time when the redemption of the world would occur. The *Apocalypse of Abraham* and the book of *Enoch* contain descriptions of the end of the world, and symbolic calculations for the date set for the redemption.[3] At that time all the secrets known only to the mystics will become universal knowledge. 'All shall be revealed!'

The belief in the coming of a Messiah is at the core of Jewish and Christian religion, and its anticipation is a powerful expectation of many people in our modern world, whether they are conscious of it or not. The historical obsession with these issues remains buried within our unconscious and informs our actions and beliefs, even if we are not aware of the influence they exert.

The Hebrew Millennium and the Jubilee Year

The number seven has many meanings within the Judeo-Christian tradition. Seven itself represents the vibration of *harmony*. In *Leviticus* 23, the first appointed feast was God's rest on the seventh day of Creation. The seven sacraments symbolize these seven days, the seven ages of man, and are reflected in the daily cycle of prayers and the yearly round of seven major religious festivals. The dates of the seven festivals are related to a musical division of the calendar in which each month is equal to a semitone of an octave.[4]

The square of seven is also used often. The harvest 'Festival of Weeks' was celebrated seven weeks (7 x 7 days) after the feast of the First Sheaf, and a sacrifice of grain was offered fifty days (one day after the seventh sabbath) after that. Shavout is the fiftieth day after Passover (the leaving of Egypt), and is one of the three major holidays each year celebrating the giving of the Ten Commandments to Moses on Mt Sinai. The date of Easter is fifty days (7 x 7 + 1) before the Pentecost. Thus seven and its powers determine the religious calendar.

The number seven was also central to the *Shemitah*, the Hebrew cyclical theory of time and history. The Jewish calendar is based on cycles of seven — the days of the week; the division of the year into seven periods of fifty days each and an additional five days; and the seven times seven days plus one of the Pentecost. The principle of seven times seven governed all history. There was a Sabbath each week, and Sabbath years every seventh year. The Sabbatical Year was an admonition to the farmers to leave their fields fallow every seventh year to rest so that they would be more fruitful, and the custom is still observed in the academic world with professors being given sabbatical years off for independent study.

Every fiftieth year was celebrated as a Jubilee Year.

And you shall count seven weeks of years, seven times seven years, so that the time of the seven weeks of years shall be to you forty-nine years . . . And you shall hallow the fiftieth year, and proclaim

liberty throughout the land to all its inhabitants; it shall be a jubilee
for you, when each of you shall return to his family. A jubilee shall
that fiftieth year be to you; in it you shall neither sow nor reap what
grows of itself, nor gather the grapes from the undressed vines. For
it shall be a jubilee; it shall be holy to you.

Leviticus, 23:8-12

The final Jubilee Cycle was seven cycles of seven thousand years each,
followed by a millennial Jubilee Year of one thousand years, corresponding to the week concluded by the Sabbath. During each of the
seven cycles the Torah is read in different ways, while the ultimate
version governs the Millennium.

In thirteenth-century Hebrew sacred texts, the world age was a
symbolic representation of the stages of a process by which all things
emanate from God and return to Him. In the following centuries it was
essential that Jewish commentators stated their belief about which
Jubilee Cycle humanity was in, and at what stage of the world cycle.
It was determined that in our age the world is governed by the
principle of stern judgment. The good news is that after the present
Shemitah ending in the year AD 2000 the Torah will no longer contain
prohibitions, evil will be curbed, and Utopia will be realized.[5] The
belief in this esoteric cycle of years is at the core of the Jewish struggle.
Underlying the history of modern Judaism is the return to Israel in
preparation for the transition to the next Shemitah.

The Jewish belief in a time cycle for all creation focused on the idea
of a Messiah, a redeemer who would appear at the end of time to
enable and enact the transition to a new world age. This utopian belief
at the core of the Judeo-Christian tradition underlies religion in the
western world. The *Zohar,* written by a medieval Jewish apocalyptic
revolutionary, prophesied a great upheaval before the creation of a
mystical Utopia at the end of time.

The Eternal World of the Greeks

The Greek vision of the world defined by Pythagoras and Plato was
a world of ideas, of eternal *archetypes* from which reality emerged as
an inferior representation or copy. The model for the world was the
action of the planets and stars in their regular courses across the

heavens. The domain of the gods and goddesses was a rational sphere where their hierarchy was assured, a fatalistic world determined by godly (planetary) actions and their equivalent reactions on Earth, expressed by mere mortals. The heavens were divine and the Earth mundane, a division that was thought to be impossible to breach.

The *Kosmos* was the divine order of the world. Its machine-like movements, regulation and sense of universal order were all very pleasing to an ancient mind used to disorder, randomness and the unexpected. The Greek view of the universe was a natural reaction to their uncertain past. But what this view granted in providing a rationale of order to the world, it also stifled because it eliminated free will or independence from the grinding inevitability of it all.

History had no beginning or end because its end inevitably led to a new beginning. According to Plato every human was eternally reborn, with unevolved souls often choosing to reincarnate in the same body again and again, despite its painful limitations, rather than risk being given a new incarnation based on the virtues and vices of this life. A strict determinism governed all life and the effect was exhilarating in its majesty, but also crushing of the human spirit. The only release was through transcendence. The Stoics in particular believed that the world repeated eternally in even its smallest detail, and argued the total acceptance of reality as it is, without struggling to change it in any way.

It is not surprising that astrology was a premier science and a foundation of the philosophy of this world view. The mathematical movements and interrelationships of the planets and signs governed and regulated the destiny of all humans. There was no escape from fate. It required resignation, but towards the end of the Graeco-Roman era, many channels of escape arose in the form of gnostic beliefs.

Roman Soothsayers

The Romans were notorious for their obsession with soothsayers. Astrology was popular in the Roman Empire and flourished under the Caesars. The astrologer Publius Figulus prophesied that the infant son of the Roman Senator Octavius would become a master of the world, and he duly became Augustus Caesar. Augustus therefore trusted astrologers and prophets. These sibyls were known to be impenetrable and devious, much like the Delphic Oracle before them, and their answers would inevitably be interpreted by great men in a way which justified their desire for power and fame.

The birth of Christ was predicted and awaited. The legend of his birth featured the three magi, the magicians or astrologers who saw the Star of Bethlehem and came to acknowledge and bring gifts to the Saviour. This aspect of Christianity was magical and appealed to the Roman population which converted to Christianity in later times. By the end of the first century AD, astrology was almost a religion among Romans, and prophecy played a major part in the development of Roman and early Christian culture, often assimilating astrological and magical ideas into its flexible structure.

Chapter Four

Christianity and the Apocalypse

Christ as the Centre of History

The rise of Christianity as a religious and secular power changed the popular conception of the world, and gave history a centre. No longer was time circular, but a finite line, beginning at Creation and ending at the Millennium. History was seen as a progression from early pre-Christian primitive states to later civilized and advanced states, culminating in the dominion of Christianity.

The Christian conception of time was a radical departure from the cyclical time of the ancient world. The Christian Gnostics believed in cyclical world ages, but the more materialistic Church hierarchy in the first centuries after Christ eliminated the Gnostic influences and replaced them with a more mundane and radically new ethical reality. The new linear view of time, time's 'arrow', was unique. Such ideas about time were characteristic of Christianity, and their acceptance required a great leap of faith for the believers.

The eternal quality of the ancient conception was lost now that the events of the world and the life of the individual all happened within linear time. Nothing was repeated, and the eternal quality was lost. The world became a unique place containing unique events, instead of a repetitive manifestation of the archetypal. Unlike the eternal world of the Greek gods and goddesses or the Hindu and Buddhist religions, *everything happened in time*. Historic events were seen to be determined by prior causes rather than divine will or expressions of the archetypal. In a way the rationale for history now existed within history rather than outside it.

The date of Christ's birth became the transition point of history. Events happened before or after Christ, expressed later by the abbreviation AD (*Anno Domini* or Year of Our Lord). This point is a fulcrum of history, and everything which preceded it was seen as a preparation for the Divine Birth.[1]

The formal designation of years as *'Anno Domini'* was proposed by Dionysus Exiguus in AD 525. Until that time the Roman calendar had been in operation in Europe. It was not until 1681 that Bossuet proposed the idea of measuring years backwards Before Christ. Previously the years before the birth of Christ were seen as being merely a prelude to the life of Christ.

The foundation of Islam by Mohammed determined the starting date for the lunar Islamic calendar. Islamic years are measured from the Hegira when Mohammed fled from Mecca to Medina on 16 July 622, which was 1 Muharram. Subsequent years are designated AH, meaning *Ab Hegira*, 'after the Flight'. The year AD 1991 is AH 1363[2] in the Islamic calendar. While most Moslems use the Western civil calendar for organizing their lives, the Islamic calendar is used for all religious and sacred purposes.

Millennial Christianity

The kingdom of glory came to pass when Jesus became the New Adam, a progressive version of the first man. The Biblical prophets had predicted all the major events of the Bible leading up to, and including, the birth of Christ. The Christian year AD 1 divides and joins together history into two periods: a preliminary period, ushered in by the Creation and the Fall, converging towards the incarnation of Christ, for which it prepares and prophesies; and a second period of restoration and accomplishment, leading to the Second Coming of Christ.[3]

In Christian terms, the birth of the world is its Fall, and the line of history leads inexorably down towards the Final Redemption predicted by the book of *Revelation*. Humanity remains eternally crucified on the cross of matter. The elimination of time's cycle and its replacement by linear time also meant that Christ lived and was crucified only once, and that we have only one life to lead in time. We must therefore seek redemption in this life rather than anticipating second chances in other incarnations. Christianity reversed its earlier philosophical foundation with regard to time and denounced reincarnation at the Fifth Ecumenical Council at Constantinople in AD 553.

Linear time puts great pressure upon Christians to seek and achieve the redemption they seek *in this life*. It also breaks the circle of eternal recurrence. The destiny of humanity is not to identify with an eternal Soul or 'Self' animating a series of temporal bodies, but a unique combination of body, soul and spirit which will be resurrected after the final redemption of the world. This concept appealed to the early Christians.

During the early centuries of Christianity a true millennial feeling came into being. The New Testament book of *Revelation* 20:4-6 authorized the belief that after his Second Coming, Christ would establish a messianic kingdom on Earth, over which he would reign for one thousand years. It stated that the inhabitants of that kingdom would be Christian martyrs, resurrected one thousand years before the general resurrection. The early Christians saw themselves as being martyrs and therefore identified with these citizens and expected the Second Coming in their lifetime.[4]

The Book of *Revelation*

> Blessed is he that readeth, and they that hear the words of this prophecy, and keep those things which are written therein: for the time is at hand.
>
> *Revelation* of John the Divine, 1,3

Ephesus and Patmos lie near each other in the eastern Aegean. Patmos is the island where John wrote the apocalyptic book of *Revelation*. Ephesus, on the Turkish coast, was a sacred city of the mystery religions, home of the Temple of Diana, focus of the secret doctrine and a laboratory from which the essence of mystic Christianity, Buddhism, Chaldean and Zoroastrian philosophy was distilled. It was reputed that the Virgin Mary spent her last days there, and that the secret tomb of St John the Divine lay under the nearby mountains.

The proximity of these two spiritual centres has occasioned the opinion that the book of *Revelation* is a foundation of esoteric and mystic Christianity as well as being a sacred book of the Eleusinian, Egyptian and Greek mystery cults. The book has elicited great controversy because of this paradox — it is simultaneously a great work of both Christian and pagan inspiration. As a result it has been interpreted in a multitude of ways, been evoked at many times and applied to events throughout history.

The *Revelation* of St John the Divine is a dramatic vision of the end of the world containing bizarre images and beings, a far cry from the sobriety of Christianity and much closer to the earlier mystery religions of the Middle East, Egypt and Greece. Briefly, it describes St John's apparition of the Alpha and the Omega, the First and the Last, amidst seven golden candlesticks and their equivalent planetary regents. The great Logos archetype is a synthesis of the ancient gods, as demonstrated by its imagery which combines Kronos, Father Time, Selene, the Moon Goddess of the seasons and the waters, and other archetypal deities. The Logos carries the keys (the planets) of life, death and rebirth in perfect knowledge of the mysteries.

The seven Churches in Asia correspond to the seven days of Creation, the seven 'root races', the chakra energy centres in the human body, and the hierarchy of spheres through which the initiate climbs before reaching the spiritual domain.

John observed a gigantic throne surrounded by twenty-four elders dressed in white and with gold crowns amidst an atmosphere of thunder and lightning. Seven lamps burned and created illumination for the Holy One, who held in his right hand a Book with seven seals, which no man or woman in Heaven or Earth was worthy to open. A lamb, symbolizing Christ and representing the first zodiac sign Aries, with seven horns and seven eyes appeared, and took the Book from God. The elders fell down in worship of God and the Lamb.

When the Book was opened and the first four seals were broken, the Four Horsemen of the Apocalypse emerged. These riders signify the four elements or the four world ages, the Yugas. The last horseman was Death, riding upon a pale horse, having domain over the last of these and a quarter of the Earth, to kill with hunger and sword.

With the opening of the fifth seal, all those who had been slain for the Word of God appeared. As the sixth seal was broken there was a fantastic earthquake, the Sun was darkened and the Moon turned red like blood. The stars of heaven fell from the sky, and every mountain and island was moved from its place. The great day of the Wrath of God had come. The angels of the wind came, and an angel sealed the foreheads of the 144,000 who should be preserved on the day of tribulation.

The seventh seal brought peace for a time, whereupon seven

Figure 3. The Day of Wrath
Illustration to *Revelation* 6, 9-16 ". . . there was a great earthquake; and the sun became black as sackcloth of hair, and the moon became as blood; and the stars fell unto the earth . . ." (Albrecht Dürer, *Apocalypse* series, 1498.)

angels emerged intoning the name of the Logos, and great catastrophes ensued. The star called Wormwood fell from the sky, symbolizing the profanity of humanity in desecrating the wisdom of God. And demons attacked all those who did not have the seal of God on their foreheads. Plagues, locusts, scorpions and hideous creatures persecuted all kinds of beings on Earth, until they wished for the release of death. Another star brought a book which it bade John eat, so that he could partake of the ancient wisdom and initiation. He was counselled, 'Thou must prophesy again before many peoples and nations and tongues and kings.' He was given a rod with which to measure the temple of God, and the altar, and those that worshipped within. And, condoning the necessity of prophecy, he gave careful instructions to save and preserve those who gave witness and prophecy.

A pregnant woman clothed with the Sun, with the Moon under her feet, wearing a crown of twelve stars on her head appeared, only to be threatened by a great red dragon with seven crowned heads. After the defeat of the dragon by St Michael, Satan arose and deceived the whole world.

Standing on the shore, John saw a beast arise from the sea with seven heads and ten horns, the Beast of the Apocalypse, whose number was 666. This creature is the Antichrist, empowered by the dragon.

Coinciding with the announcement of the fall of Babylon, the city of confusion, the Lamb was seen with the 144,000 saved ones. This multitude observed others dying and suffering from the trials and tribulations of sin. Then seven angels signifying the Pleiades appeared and gave their sacred vials to the Earth with the seven plagues, whereupon the scarlet woman, the Harlot of Babylon, seated on a beast, rose with a cup of abominations. The angels blasphemed God and destroyed the Earth and its peoples.

The final omnipotence of God prevailed, and the marriage of the Lamb ensued. John fell at the feet of the Lamb, who said to him, 'Worship God: for the testimony of Jesus is the spirit of prophecy.' A white horse materialized, surmounted by the word of God, followed by the armies of God clothed in white. Written on his armour was 'King of Kings and Lord of Lords'. The armies made war against the beast, slew him and bound Satan for a thousand years, on the provision that after this time he would be free again.

John saw the dead, small and great, stand before God, and the Book of Life was opened, and the dead were judged according to their works guided by the Book. Those that did not deserve to be resurrected were cast into a lake of fire, the second death.

Finally he saw a new heaven and a new Earth, for the old heaven and Earth had perished. The holy city of Jerusalem was prepared as a bride for her husband. And God said to him, 'I am the Alpha and the Omega, the beginning and the end.'

The city of Jerusalem was described in great detail, together with the twelve angels of the gates of the city, corresponding to the twelve tribes of Israel, and the measurements and proportions of the city.

In the centre of the city was the River of Life, clear as crystal, proceeding out from the throne of God and the Lamb.

In the midst of the street of it, and on either side of the river, was there the tree of life, which bare twelve manner of fruits, and yielded the fruit every month: and the leaves of the tree were for the healing of the nations. And he said unto me, These sayings are faithful and true. And the Lord God of the holy prophets sent his angel to show unto his servants the things which must shortly be done.[5]

The prophecies of the book of *Revelation* finish with the Grace of God.

The prophecy of *Revelation* is highly suggestive, and the destruction of the world is relevant to our current age as well as to those early Christians two thousand years ago. The primary lesson is that God rewards goodness and condemns evil. What is disputed is the timing of the millennium of peace and the general attribution of the images to events on Earth.

Millennial Cults

There were many similar Apocalypses written in the years after Christ. Among these are a bewildering number of apocryphal texts eliminated from the orthodox New Testament by the early Church Fathers.

The *Apocalypse of Thomas* states that the Apostle Thomas was told by Jesus that the period of time from his ascension into heaven to the second advent would be comprised of nine jubilees. Among the interesting prophecies made in this book are:

> On a sudden there shall arise near the last time a king, a lover of the law, who shall hold rule not for long: he shall leave two sons. The first is named of the first letter (A), the second of the eighth (H). The first shall die before the second.
>
> Thereafter shall arise two princes to oppress the nations, under whose hands there shall be a very great famine in the right-hand part of the east, so that nation shall rise up against nation and be driven out from their own borders.[6]

The book continues to describe floods preventing communication, the deaths of all those east of Babylon, and then the seven signs which will foretell the end of the world. There will be sharing between kings, voices echoing from the firmament, and catastrophes of pestilence and hunger on Earth. Upon the completion of these acts, the elect will be delivered to the throne of God, there to rest in eternity.

Other apocrypha such as the *Apocalypse of the Virgin*, the *Revelation of Stephen*, the *Apocalypse of Peter* and the *Apocalypse of Paul*, are all generally similar in style and content to John's book of *Revelation*. These other books contain more gnostic influences than the accepted version of John, and read more like early versions of Dante's *Inferno* than a Biblical apocalypse. In the *Apocalypse of Paul*, in particular, many places in Hell and Paradise are visited, and the educational qualities useful for conversion are more pronounced. The alternative apocrypha which were written from one to three centuries after John's continued to be very popular.

Since its time, the book of *Revelation* has been taken literally and interpreted symbolically. In AD 156, Montanus declared himself an incarnation of the Holy Ghost and predicted that he would reveal the true message mentioned in the *Revelation* — that the creation of the New Jerusalem was at hand. Thousands of Montanists went to Phrygia to await the Second Coming, fasting and praying with bitter repentance.[7] They were only the first of many to respond and act in accordance with the prophecies of this powerful book.

Many people have predicted and prophesied the time of the

apocalypse as described in the book of *Revelation*. Predictions from the years after it was written projected an end far beyond the lifetime of those then alive, which was the safest time frame to use.

Some determined the time of the apocalypse by using numerology. The book of *Revelation* has many numbers, and their significance has not escaped those willing to investigate them. For a while, the year 666 was a favourite date, derived from the *gematria* of the name of the beast of the apocalypse, whose number it states as six hundred, threescore and six. Gematria was the conversion of a name into a number by making each letter in the Greek alphabet correspond to a number. The letters in the name in Greek are added up, and their significance is deciphered. This figure yielded the 666 date.

Some believed that the year AD 365 would be the end of the world, while others accepted the Grand Climacteric of AD 6300, or the gigantic numbers in *Chronicles* 21.

However, by the time of St Augustine in the fourth century AD, astrology was outlawed as another heretical cult by the ascendant Christians. Although Augustine had been interested in astrology as a young man, he later had theological difficulties with the idea that planets could control one's destiny.

Augustine condemned astrology and prophecy on the doubtful logic that planetary influences usurped God's power, but in the process gave the planets a great effect and importance. This affected the judgments of the Church for many centuries, and prophecy fell into disrepute as a result.

In his great work, *The City of God*, Augustine stated that the book of *Revelation* was to be understood as a spiritual allegory and that the Millennium was already realized within the Church and had started with the Crucifixion. As a result of his views, which were immediately accepted, all subsequent millennial statements were viewed with suspicion as being unorthodox, if not heretical. But pious Christians continued to see themselves as members of the elect, rather than as minions of the devil who would be cast out. They were the Chosen People of the Lord.

The Sibylline Oracles

During the late stages of the Roman Empire the *Sibylline Oracles* provided a fictional resurrection of millennial feeling.[8] Originally written as inspired writings in Greek to convert pagans to Judaism, they enjoyed a great popularity. The Christians of the time noticed how successful they were and adapted versions for themselves. The hero of the Oracles was the Christ of the book of *Revelation* — the warrior Christ fighting the Devil.

The Christian Sibyllines proclaimed the Emperor Constantine as a messianic king and adopted a mystical approach to the succession of emperors which followed him. A sibylline oracle called the *Tiburtina* described the exploits of a mythic hero, the Emperor of the Last Days, a knight who did battle with the Antichrist. The story described an Emperor who converted the heathen, destroyed the temples of false gods and baptized the converted. Upon the conversion of the Jews themselves, the Holy Sepulchre shone in glory. When he had accomplished his task he retired to Golgotha, laid down his sword and dedicated his kingdom to God.

In the midst of this idyllic scene, the Antichrist took over the Temple of Jerusalem and deceived the ignorant with his miracles and fake acts of piety. The Lord saw the dilemma, shortened the time period of the millennium and sent Archangel Michael to destroy the Antichrist. Once this had been done, the Millennium of Peace began. The story is typical of sibylline oracles of the time and one can see why they were so popular.

Other prophecies were even more outrageous and reconstructed times back in history to Eden and forward to future times with godly kings, reminiscent of King Arthur or Charlemagne, fighting the Antichrist until the Last Judgment. The popularly produced *Sibylline Oracles* were almost as well known as the Bible and had a great influence on the population. Like Nostradamus' books later, they were continually translated, reprinted, adapted, modified and republished for ever greater and wider audiences. Generation after generation anxiously awaited the appearance of the horned Antichrist emerging to attempt to conquer the Christian world. It probably aided the legend that the great cathedrals used such millennial imagery in their rose windows and carvings to appeal to the populace.

Figure 4. The New Jerusalem Revealed to St John
Statan begins his one-thousand-year sentence in the Abyss.
(Albrecht Dürer, *Apocalypse* series, 1498.)

The Millennium Year AD 1000

The only date mentioned in the book of *Revelation* is the year AD
1000. Many theories attempted to justify this date, and to many the

year one thousand was 'The Year'. In the tenth century, Christianity was still a persecuted creed and there was little hope for the kind of ultimate triumph indicated in the New Testament. Faithful Christians believed and anticipated that in the year 1000 they would witness the 'Second Coming' of Christ, the 'New Jerusalem' and the beginning of Christ's Millennial Reign — a great and glorious time in which the good Christians of the world would live in peace and prosperity, while the infidels and the damned would be condemned to Hell.

Christianity gained in popularity due to the imminent coming of the Millennium, which became the most effective recruiting device since martyrdom. There were many pro-millennial sects, often composed of uncertain believers somewhere between Judaism and Christianity, such as the Ebonists, the Montanists and others. Belief in the Millennium became a central point in their religious articles of faith. Others, such as the Gnostics, neo-Platonists and even St Augustine were against the concept of the Millennium. The Bishops of the Church found the whole idea a bit tasteless, as they were expected to condemn the first thousand years of their predecessors' Christian rule as disastrous, sinful, and justifying a conclusion of doom and destruction.

As the Millennium year approached, zealots took extreme measures to prepare for the end of the world. In the year 971 a lease was made for exactly twenty-nine years.[9] There was a flurry of church-building, of donations to the church authorities, and an influx of conversions as the time approached. The whole world waited and trembled for the coming of the end. All over the European world Saracens, Vikings and Huns invaded, taking a few hostages, but no dragons flew down from the skies nor did rivers turn to blood, nor devils roam the countryside. The year 1000 dawned and then passed, and the End did not happen.

Redefining the Millennium

The true believers moved the goalposts further ahead. They reasoned that one thousand years should have been measured not from the birth of Christ, but from the Crucifixion in AD 33. Therefore a new millennial time of 1033 was proposed, offering new chances for the drama of salvation. Again it was all in vain. The only people who benefited were those who became more attracted to magic than worship as a result of the let-down.

The famous Conquest Comet of 1066 foretold the death of England, which turned out to be correct because of the successful Norman conquests which culminated in that year. England would never be the same again.

There were a succession of other years when eminent authorities projected the Apocalypse. One was the year 1496, which apparently had sound astrological backing, and during which a creature was fished out of the Tiber in Rome, a monster with a donkey's head, a maiden's body, a stag's right foot, a griffin's left, and an old grey face instead of a rump — but the year ended like all the others, with no notable occurrences.

Pseudo-Methodius discovered a rich source of numerological prophecy in the *Sibylline Leaves*. St Vincent of Ferrier believed that the number of verses in the book of *Psalms* could be the key, and therefore prophesied the year 2537 as the Millennium.

The month of February 1524 was propitious, and Stoffler thought that the conjunction of Saturn, Mars and Jupiter in Pisces, the Fishes, signalled the right time. Some made arks and prepared for the worst. Alas, the floods never came.

In 1583 Bishop Jewel noted that there had been a vogue for prophecies of the Millennium during the previous two hundred years, and that Doomsday was most likely to be linked with a series of symbolic events such as the conversion of the Turks, the fall of Rome, or the return of Christ and the Saints. Such speculations were taken seriously by historians, scholars, and theologians and it seemed that everyone had millennial expectations of one kind or another. Thomas mentions that in May 1643 Parliamentary troops in the Wallingford area were told that Christ was coming to destroy Charles I, and that the Earl of Essex was John the Baptist.[10]

By the year 1649, there were said to have been more than eighty books written on the subject.[11] The year 1656 was popular for a while, because that was believed to be the number of years elapsed between the Creation and the Flood.

The year 1666 was a likely year of the Great Beast of the Apocalypse, being 1000 + 666, and was the next target for the millennial devotees, but the Great Fire of London, while a considerable tragedy, was the only newsworthy event, and hardly qualified for the end of the world.

William Sedgwick, the preacher of Ely Cathedral, went to London with the news that the world would end within fourteen days because Christ had appeared in his study and had told him so. Millenarian groups became so prominent in politics and religion that they became much more than mere cranks raving about the end of the world; they were a political force to be reckoned with. Prophecy was a central aspect of their religion and to lack an opinion about when the End would come amounted to a serious lack of understanding of the world.

Even as late as 1707 three French prophets were thrown into jail for announcing that the Last Days had begun, and in the same year over 400 people were known to be prophesying in various parts of the country. By the latter stages of the eighteenth century, however, it was considered a sign of mental illness to prophesy or to believe in prophecies.

The Julian Calendar had been instituted in the time of Julius Caesar, and by the late sixteenth century had become ten days out of synchronization with the actual times of the equinoxes and solstices. This occurred because the Julian calculation of the length of the year was inaccurate by eleven minutes, an error which accumulated at the rate of one and a half days in 200 years. Pope Gregory took action and eliminated ten days from the calendar, and ruled that in the future Gregorian calendar every century year would not be a leap year unless divisible by 400. When the changes were instituted in England in 1752, 3 September of that year became 14 September, to the amazement of the people, who did not understand the reasons for the change. There were demonstrations, and angry people shouted, 'Give us back our eleven days!'[12]

The Gnosis of Resurrection

The idea of the Millennium implies a forced return to the rule of God, manifest for Christians through the Second Coming of Jesus Christ, or for Islamic sects such as the Ismailis and Mazdaeans, the Last Imam who will usher out the dying world and introduce the New Age. The Ismailis believed that there have been 18,000 worlds before ours, and that in the 'original world', as well as in each of the subsequent world ages, there was a race derived from the Adam of the Bible and the Koran.

Adam is simultaneously the last survivor of each outgoing world age and the prophet and initiator of the new incoming world order. In what is called the 'Unveiling of the Gnosis of Resurrection,'[13] present day humanity dimly echoes the perfection of earlier ages and yet must return from ignorance and reclaim the wonder and power of heaven. We are considered to be degenerate and must achieve redemption by reclaiming our lost understanding before the end of the world, at all costs. It is the function of the Imam to guide the process of awakening humanity. Adam knows the external laws and their meanings, while the eternal Eve understands the esoteric and hidden meanings of transcendence. All imams are reflections of the eternal Imam, a reflection of Adam. The end of a world age is a time when the integration of masculine and feminine happens, and when the power of time will be defeated.

The Last Judgment

Jewish, Christian, Native American and many other religious teachings assert that a Messiah will come to Earth. They also prophesy specific physical events which will announce and accompany the appearance of the Messiah. One such signal for his appearance is an increase in the severity of earthquakes and other natural disturbances.

According to the Bible, nations will rise against each other, and earthquakes will hit humanity, the shockwaves of which will shift the Earth on its very axis. Mountains will move, cities disappear and major geographical events will announce and accompany the coming of the Messiah. The fifth-century prophet Zachariah referred to a battle, an Armageddon, when earthquakes will split the Mount of Olives in two. There are many references to increasing cold and a lack of light, and a similar chain of events is described in *Luke,* 21:11 and *Revelation,* 16:18.

The idea of a Last Judgment is a powerful aspect of Christianity, Islam, Buddhism and Hinduism. At the end of a world age, the influences of eternity meet, and it therefore contains the implication of the rebirth of the world on a higher level. The Egyptians believed that from living a life free of evil, the soul would become Osiris, that is, enter the domain of heaven. The belief in achieving salvation through the Last Judgment is an archetypal expression. The process experienced by an individual soul at death is a mirror of the process experienced by all souls at the Last Judgment of humanity, at the end of a world age, at the Millennium.

Russian Judgment icons depict the multitudes of humanity watching over the judgment of a soul, weighed by scales held by the hand of God. When the impulse to wisdom and regeneration are dominant, the soul ascends to heaven, but if the lower desires of materialism, sexuality and greed dominate, the soul descends into hell. The snake, symbolizing time, stretches from the lowest reaches of hell to the highest reaches of heaven, into the presence of Christ.

The fifteenth century woodcut of St Michael slaying the dragon of time also shows him holding a scales, weighing the souls of the dead. At the end of time humanity is judged and balances exacted, as in Egyptian iconography and Tibetan Buddhism. In Tibetan Buddhism the soul is torn apart or eaten by demons, incinerated in eternal fires and subjected to extreme forces and trials, the passage of which determines the quality of the next incarnation. Only the submission to transcendent consciousness eliminates the cycles of incarnations altogether.

The belief in the Millennium and its associated Last Judgment is at the core of the major world religions, and within the collective consciousness. As individuals we seek such a release and rebirth, and there are signals which lead us to assume that we are heading towards a time which has been prophesied for many centuries — a time of universal judgment and salvation. Among the many sources of historical prophecy are the famous monuments of Egypt.

Figure 5. St Michael Slaying the Dragon and Weighing Souls
Michael was the leader of the forces of light which routed the Devil
in the war of heaven, symbolic of the victory of the spirit over the
lower nature of man. As he conquers the dragon, he also weighs the
souls of the dead at the Last Judgment. (15th century German
woodcut.)

Chapter Five

Prophecies of the Great Pyramid

The Great Pyramid contains:

> The wisdom and acquirements in the different arts and sciences
> ... the sciences of arithmetic and geometry, that they might remain
> as records for the benefit of those who would afterwards compre-
> hend them ... the positions of the stars and their cycles, together
> with the history and chronicle of time past, of that which is to come,
> and every future event which would take place in Egypt.
>
> from the *Akhbar-Ezzeman Coptic MS.*[1]

The Great Pyramid has exerted a fascination for at least the past four
thousand years. The accepted archaeological view of the Great
Pyramid is that it was built around 2170 BC as the burial tomb of the
Pharaoh Cheops. While no remains have ever been discovered within
the King's Chamber, located two-thirds of the way from the massive
base to the top, some hieroglyphs found on a cartouche there do refer
to Cheops. The most sensible theory is that Cheops had them
inscribed when he appropriated the monument as his tomb.

It has been suggested that the pyramid was designed by the
legendary architect Imhotep, who was the Egyptian Great Architect,
the God of Healing and the originator of the Masonic Mysteries which
culminated in the cathedral builders in the eleventh century AD.

The Great Pyramid also could be thousands of years older than we
believe, a reminder of Atlantean times long since passed, when
humanity possessed a more spiritual reality than today. If it predated
the Egyptians themselves, it would have been even more of a mystery
to them as to us.

The pyramid is 481 feet (146.6m) high and is constructed from thousands of blocks of limestone, each weighing from two to ten tons. The pyramid was originally faced with brilliant white stones, probably alabaster or marble, all of which have long since been removed. When the pyramid was built, it must have been truly awe-inspiring, glistening in the sun.

The organization and effort required to quarry the stones from the ground, lift them out, shape them, transport them miles from their quarries, and then to raise them to their location in the pyramid is almost beyond comprehension. It would have taken thousands of workers more than a lifetime to construct this first of the Seven Wonders of the ancient world. Even the most optimistic estimates of the time taken to build the pyramid would have exceeded the length of Cheops' life — a fact which effectively sabotages the conventional archaeological theory of the pyramid as a burial chamber. Modern engineers have stated that it would be virtually impossible to construct such a monument today, despite the sopisticated machinery available.

A Short History of Pyramidology

The mute silence of the Great Pyramid testifies to the advanced state of what is still considered by many to be a 'primitive' civilization. Theories to explain its construction and purpose have puzzled and stimulated great minds. Trivial and mundane, traditional archaeological theory maintains that the monument was the burial chamber of a megalomaniac pharaoh, and that the significant proportions, measurements and more arcane characteristics ascribed to the pyramid were accidental.

When Herodatus visited the pyramids in 500 BC, classical Egyptian civilization was already in decline. He was astounded by tales told by the pyramid guides, apparently mistaking them for priests. The tales told of Atlantean civilization to Plato in his journeys to Egypt also fired an interest in the legendary creators of Egyptian civilization and the builders of the pyramid.

The artists of Napoleon's Egyptian invasion in 1792 created wonderful line illustrations of the pyramids and other antiquities, which bewitched the European public with the Egyptian mysteries.

The curiosity over Egyptian matters increased with the discovery and deciphering of the Rosetta Stone by Champollion in 1822. The Rosetta Stone has the same inscription written in Greek, Demotic, and hieroglyphs which, for the first time, permitted a translation of hieroglyphs. Before then scholars had supposed that the Egyptian civilization had been of a high order, but the mundane translations of the hieroglyphs portrayed a boastful and banal people. The translators could not understand why such an advanced culture appeared to have used such an incoherent language. They never considered that the language could have a symbolic significance which escaped them, and which still eludes the traditional Egyptology establishment.[2]

The Western esoteric schools have accepted the Great Pyramid as a centre for initiation and a symbol of the potency of esoteric thought in the ancient world. Madame Blavatsky, Edgar Cayce, Alice Bailey and Rudolf Steiner, among others, believed the original Egyptians to be survivors from the doomed Atlantis. The flawed, but high Atlantean civilization was characterized by an integration of spiritual and physical power, but the base materialism of the people destroyed the civilization and its island capital, leading to its sinking beneath the Atlantic Ocean. The survivors of the cataclysm which destroyed Atlantis spread and settled in Peru, Egypt, Mexico, and Central, South and North America, explaining why these cultures share a common iconography and also flood and Atlantis legends. This idea is one variation of pyramid interpretation.

During the nineteenth century the pyramids were studied obsessively by a succession of highly religious men, verging on the fanatical, who claimed to have discovered mystical messages within its geometry and dimensions. In 1859, the fundamentalist Christian astronomer John Taylor challenged contemporary theories by identifying the dimensions of the pyramid as mathematical keys to knowledge of the Earth and its relationship to the cosmos. Because he could not explain its obviously non-Christian origin, he was forced to postulate divine revelation for its inspiration.

Surveys undertaken by Professor Piazzi Smyth in 1864-5 confirmed Taylor's mathematics and measurements, including his hypothesis of a 'polar inch' as the primary unit of measurement. In the process he produced carefully measured drawings of the entire system of internal passages and wall surfaces and published a complete record of the internal and external geometry of the pyramid. These measurements allowed later researchers to form and substantiate their theories.

Great Pyramid Prophecies

In 1865, Robert Menzies first advanced the theory that the proportions and measurements of the passage system of the Great Pyramid were a chronological representation of a prophecy, even though nothing was known about Egyptian messianic prophecies at the time. By equating the polar inch with the solar year, he reasoned that the Grand Gallery was the Christian Dispensation, beginning with the birth of Christ. He subsequently advanced the idea that the entrance doorway of the Antechamber symbolized the beginning of the final period of the great wars and tribulations prophesied in the Bible.

There followed a great debate among dedicated churchmen and pyramidologists over the exact dates of the beginning of the Great Dispensation, whether it began with the Nativity or the Crucifixion. Among the most scholarly works about these ideas was *The Great Pyramid: Its Divine Message* by Davidson and Aldersmith, published in 1925, which sought to demonstrate that:

1.   The Great Pyramid is a geometrical representation of the mathematical basis of the science of high Egyptian civilization.
2.   The builders had condensed an understanding of natural law into a general formula analogous to Einstein's Relativity Theory.
3.   The formula affected all Egyptian art, literature, religion and ethics.
4.   The Cheops pyramid was the 'standard pyramid' upon which others were based and against which they were compared.
5.   The passage system graphically represents an elaborate prophetic chronology intimately related to Biblical prophecy, which gives various essential dates for the Christian Dispensation and accurately predicts the precise dates for the beginning and end of World War I.
6.   Pyramid symbolism in conjunction with Biblical prophecy indicates a message addressed to the present era and that the Time of Tribulation prophesied in the Bible was the twentieth century.[3]

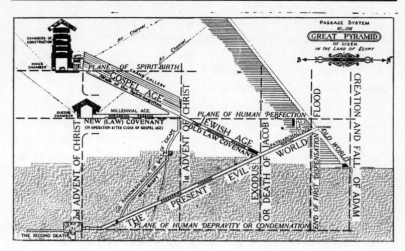

Figure 6. The Great Pyramid Chart of the Ages
The passage system of the Great Pyramid analysed and measured to
show the dating system from the Creation of Adam to the Plane of
Spirit Birth at the King's Chamber. (Edgar, *The Great Pyramid: Its
Time Features*, 1924.)

The accompanying diagram illustrates the hypothesis that the Passion
of the Messiah had been predicted three thousand years before the
Birth of Christ, when the pyramid was originally built. Davidson
maintained that the 'Great Step' between the intersection of 'The Hall
of Truth in Darkness' (The First Ascending Passage) and 'The Hall of
Truth in Light' (The Grand Gallery), signified the interval of thirty-
three years between the birth of Christ and His crucifixion in AD 33.

In the *Great Pyramid Passages,* John and Morton Edgar defined the
symbolism of the passageways of the Great Pyramid, a scheme which
Davidson followed.[4] In their model the various passages and chambers were related to stages in Christian history:

1.   Descending Passage to the subterranean chamber - the world
on its downward course since the Adamic condemnation.
2.   Ascending Passage — the Dispensation of the Israelites to the
Law for 1647 years, beginning with the Exodus from Egypt in 1615
BC and ending with the crucifixion of Christ in AD 33. This
symbolized an elongated life with earthly blessings, while after
Christ a spiritual life with heavenly blessings was ordained. The

granite plugs which blocked the entrance to the ascending passage represent the Divine Law, terminating the validity of the Covenant of the Jews.

3.   Horizontal Passage to the Queen's Chamber — symbolized perfect human life and nature at the end of Christ's millennial reign. As such it represented the potential for eternal life in perfection.

4.   The Well — symbolizing Hades, the state of death from which the Awakening will emerge, represented by the Death and Resurrection of Christ. Its shaft shows the only way to immortality because the ascending passageway is blocked by the plugs of the Covenant.

5.   Grand Gallery — the Gospel Dispensation of grace indicating the advent of Jesus Christ.

6.   King's Chamber — the heavenly inheritance of immortality experienced by those who possess the divine nature and have responded to enjoin the covenant with God to follow Christ.

7.   The Antechamber — the School of Christ.

8.   The last three represent the highest level of spiritual attainment possible on the earthly plane.

Christ's Millennial Reign

The Great Pyramid: Its Time Features describes Morton Edgar's Pyramid scheme, the dating of which culminated in the year 1915. He felt that this date signified the entrance of humanity on to the 'Plane of Human Perfection,' when the invisible Jesus Christ exercised his divinely conferred right and assumed kingly authority as the humanity's new invisible ruler.[5] By careful measurement, he determined that the 1915 pyramid inches of the Grand Gallery represent the time from the birth of Jesus Christ to the year 1914. This measurement brings us to the level of the King's Chamber and symbolizes his entrance as King of Israel and the world. Edgar's quite optimistic prophecies were presented as a turning point in human history.

Edgar also identified a 2915-year time period which implied a different perspective on religious and mundane history. As Nostradamus had before him, Edgar accepted a six-thousand-year duration for the 'Present Evil World,' followed by a one thousand year 'Millennial Age'. He dated the Creation of Adam and the world at 4128 BC and

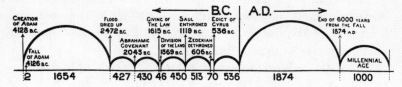

Figure 7. The Millennial Age
The entire dating of history from the Creation of Adam in 4128 BC,
to the end of 6,000 years from the Fall, and the 1,000-year Millennial
Age. (Edgar, The Great Pyramid: Its Time Features, 1924.)

the Fall of Adam at 4126 BC in conformance with Bishop Ussher,
therefore the period of six thousand years before the beginning of the
Millennial Age would end in the year 1874. The addition of the one-
thousand-year Millennial Age would date the end of the world at AD
2874.

The Horizontal Passage which leads to the Queen's Chamber is
symbolic of the 'Millennial Reign of Jesus Christ', and the length of the
two Ascending Passages the duration of the Law and Gospel Ages,
combining for a complete period of 7000 years. At the culmination of
this time God would punish evildoers and reward the righteous
because of their faith in Him. God 'hath appointed a day in which he
will judge the world in righteousness by that man whom he hath
ordained', the Lord Jesus Christ. The 'day' he appointed will be the
seventh 1000-year period since the time of Adam. During this time
humanity will experience the effects of divine grace, in contrast to the
evil of the preceding six 1000-year periods. The entire period was
designed by God for humanity's ultimate and everlasting benefit, that
they might learn good from evil, so as to be able to choose
righteousness and life.

The Horizontal Passage to the Queen's Chamber illustrates the
hopeful condition of humanity. Because the first six-sevenths of the
passage is only four feet (1.1m) high, it forces a man or woman of
average stature to walk stooped over. This is symbolic of the
subjection of humanity, labouring under sin and degradation, and its
longing for the promised deliverance. The deliverance will take place
during the seventh 1000-year period, 'the time for the restitution of all
things.' At this point the passage drops twenty-one inches, and
allowing greater freedom of movement, represents the greater

freedom of the Millennial Age. The original Adamic condemnation will be removed and the new Covenant established. This hell and brimstone talk is typical of the commentators of the Pyramid and their millennial and apocalyptic Christianity.

Edgar dated the end of the period for the final test of humanity as AD 2914, which will be 2915 years from the birth of Jesus Christ. But he also sees a different timetable for the freeing of the disobedient and more primitive Adamic energy. Adam reaches the twenty-fifth course of the Pyramid, symbolizing the 'Plane of Human Perfection,' at the end of seven thousand years, and, losing hold of his formerly perfect state, falls into the Descending Passage condition of death. If Christ is the whole Pyramid, Adam is his pre-spiritual counterpart. Adam and Christ are the only two who stand upon the 'Plane of Human Perfection,' though Adam fell through his disobedience.

Christ's 'Day of Restitution' will occur in the year 2874, when the world will have regained all it has lost. Added to this are a 'little season' of forty years, during which God will destroy those secretly harbouring the spirit of the adversary Satan, along with Satan, in a 'Second Death' as described in *Revelation* 20:1-3 and *Psalms* 37:10. Those that pass the final test will have proven that they have developed the perfect character of the Redeemer. Thus, according to Edgar, the entire period of 7040 years takes us through the ages of the world.

Edgar's scheme is based on the measurements of Piazzi Smyth, but he does not provide any specific events between the years 1915 and 2874. While his model is quite extraordinary in its attention to detail in most respects, the lack of such events in modern times is a shortcoming, and emphasizes the fact that his historical perspective extends no further than the Bible.

The Final Tribulation

The dates contained in the passageways leading to the King's Chamber and its Antechamber have been studied in extreme detail because they are attributed to the years from 1909 to 1953. So precise was the correlation of Davidson's inch-equals-one-year dating with Piazzi Smyth's measurements that they defined a series of important dates relating to political, economic and social changes during the forty-four years, dated to the nearest day. Davidson identified the exact dates of the beginning and end of the First World War, and accurately predicted the month of the beginning of the Second World War in 1939. Davidson was not only precise about retrospective dating of the Great Pyramid's passageways, but was also very specific about the prophecies he saw indicated in the future.

In Davidson's chronology, the Second Low Passage between the Antechamber and the King's Chamber corresponded to 'The Final Tribulation' between 1928 and 1936, which closely correlates with the New York Stock Market Crash of 1929 and the Great Depression which followed during the 1930s.

The time scale extended to 1953, when Davidson believed an event would happen which would forever alter the face of the world. This date roughly coincided with the testing of the first hydrogen bomb and the outbreak of the Korean War, the first of which could be said to be momentous in every way.

Max Toth projected that the end of the Pyramid's recorded time falls between July 1992 and September 2001, developed by extending a vertical line from the end of the King's Chamber to its intersection with the subterranean chamber complex, and measuring from this intersection point to the termination of the blind passageway. This time corresponds to a 'phase of ending' of our world cycle.[6] A Kingdom of the Spirit will emerge between 1995 and 2025 with higher spiritual goals and ethics, but associated natural storms and eruptions will have become an accepted fact of life. The final collapse of civilization will be in 2025, after which a new society will be created.

The rebirth of the new society will be heightened when a sign of the Messiah's appearance will be seen in the sky in the year 2034, followed in 2040 by Christ's physical reincarnation. From 2055 to 2080, material progress will reawaken with the expanded growth of humanity and its achievements. In 2116 the Messiah will pass away, but he will incarnate again in 2135, and yet again in 2265. According to Rutherford, the last date indicated in the Great Pyramid is AD 2979.

Figure 8. Nostradamus at the Age of Fifty-Nine.
(16th century print.)

Chapter Six

Nostradamus and the *Centuries*

There is hope that by the lapse of time, and after my extinction here on Earth, my writings will be more valued than during my lifetime.
from the *Epistle to Henry II* by Nostradamus

Nostradamus was born Michel de Nostredame in 1503 in Provence, and is the most popular, famous and enigmatic prophet in recent history. Hundreds of books have been written about his *Centuries,* a series of 942 enigmatic predictive quatrains, first published in 1555. It has been translated and reprinted in so many editions that it and the Bible are the only books to have been continuously in print since its publication.[1]

Nostradamus was a highly learned man for his time, as though destined to play the role of healer and prophet that he assumed so naturally. It was reputed that he was of Jewish descent, yet his family had converted to Christianity. Nostradamus claimed to be descended from one of the ten lost tribes of Israel, the Issachari, who were noted for their prophetic gifts. They were astrologers because they were 'men that had understanding of the times, to know what Israel ought to do.' (*Chronicles I,* 12:32) He even claimed to possess the skills of the three magi who had foretold the birth of Christ fifteen centuries earlier.

Many of Nostradamus' maternal and paternal ancestors were skilled mathematicians and doctors. He was informally educated by his grandfather, a doctor and master of the celestial science of astrology, and subsequently studied humanities at Avignon, and the theory of medicine and philosophy at Montpelier, the most famous medical school in France. After travelling for some years because the plague visited his university town, he returned to receive his degree.

He practised medicine at Toulouse and Agen, and his first marriage to a wealthy young beauty ended unfortunately when their two children died young, followed by his wife's death a few years later. He was recruited to combat the plague at Aix, which he did successfully. Upon retiring to Salon de Craux, he married again and had a daughter and three sons, and it was to his youngest son Caesar that he dedicated his books of prophecies.

The chaos and great changes happening in Europe at the time affected him deeply, and he initially composed the prophetic quatrains for his own interest. Only later did he decide to ignore the potentially unfavourable publicity by publishing them. He had practised divination techniques for many years, modified by his experience with the alliance of astrology and medicine. He believed that astrology was required by doctors, and produced almanacs so that doctors could have the advantage of accurate astrological data. As the popular almanacs of the time included predictions for the coming year, they became a proving ground for Nostradamus. He was instantly accepted as a master of prediction and prophecy, yet he was also branded as a charlatan.

His prophecies are extremely difficult to interpret because they were written in an enigmatic combination of French, its Provençal dialect, Latin, Greek and Italian, and their time sequence was consciously jumbled so that their chronology and meaning would not be revealed to the unwise. This device also protected Nostradamus from possible repercussions over his prophecies. Ever since his time, people of many generations have seen the relevance of the quatrains.

The Notorious Prediction

His most famous prediction led to an acknowledgement by the Queen of France, Catherine de Medici, wife of King Henri II. After the publication of the first seven *Centuries* in 1555, he was invited by the Queen to present himself at court on 16 August 1556. Those of his prophecies which were in vogue with courtiers involved not only the King himself (I,35), but also his seven children.

The Queen spent two hours with Nostradamus[2] and asked him

about a particular quatrain predicting the King's death, but the King himself was uninterested. The fated *Century* I,35 states:

> The young lion will overcome the older one,
> in a field of combat in single fight:
> He will pierce his eyes in their golden cage;
> two wounds in one, then he dies a cruel death.[3]

Catherine wished Nostradamus to elaborate this quatrain for her particularly because King Henri had been warned many years earlier by the Italian prophet and astrologer Luc Gauric that both the beginning and the end of his reign would be marked by duels. It was obvious that the king did not take these prophecies seriously because during the celebrations for the marriage of his sister Elizabeth to Philip II of Spain, and of his daughter Marguerite to the Duke of Savoy in 1559, he fought jousts on all three days.

During a return bout on the third day, he and Captain Montgomery engaged lances and one part of the captain's splintered shaft pierced the king's helmet and entered his head just above the eye. A second splinter wounded him in the throat. The king died after spending ten days in agony. In agreement with the prophecy the captain, who was younger than Henri, also used the lion as an emblem. Nostradamus' prediction was so precise that it was rumoured that he had participated in a plot to kill the King. He was so accurate in this and other predictions about the royal family of the time that as his notoriety grew, he quite sensibly spent the remaining years of his life very quietly, away from the cities.

During the next seven years the gout and ill health which had plagued his latter years became steadily worse until it turned to dropsy. Realizing the end was near, Nostradamus made his will on 17 June 1566, leaving 3,444 gold crowns above his other possessions. On the morning of 2 July 1566, the exact date which he himself had predicted for his death, he was found dead.

Nostradamus' Prophetic Techniques

Nostradamus possessed a fantastic historical insight which, through an amalgam of his powers and abilities, has fascinated people for almost five centuries. He was a gifted mathematician, doctor and astrologer, but also possessed prophetic powers which he could summon at will. His prophecies are an unusual blend of the scientific and the supernatural, the clear and the obtuse, the specific and the mythical.

Because he described events taking place far into the future, which he apparently saw clearly, it is only natural that he used unusual descriptive words which do not make much sense today. Thus he talked about flying insects and birds when he could have meant aeroplanes, great raging fires which could be nuclear weapons, and used cities, states, and personages from the past to describe future behaviour and events. In his usage, warlike cities behaved like Sparta; and royal birds may be the eagles used by the Romanovs, the German aristocracy or the USA to denote their superiority.

He used astrological terms to refer to events and people, such as Neptune when referring to naval battles or Turkish fleets, Mars when describing warriors, Sol or the Sun when portraying kings and Luna or the Moon when referring to queens or powerful women, and Islamic influences.

Prophets were still persecuted in Nostradamus' time, and he was very careful about being too specific. There was always the danger that people in important places would think his prophecies pertained to them and take offence. Nostradamus protected himself with poetic, obscure and alliterative devices.

In the first two quatrains of *Century* I, Nostradamus described his divination techniques:

Sitting alone at night in secret study;
it is placed on the brass tripod.
A slight flame comes out of the emptiness and
makes successful that which should not be believed in vain.

Century I,1

and,

The wand in the hand is placed between the tripod's legs.
With water he sprinkles the hem of his garment and his foot.
A voice, fear; he trembles in his robes.
Divine splendour; the god sits nearby.[4]

Century I,2

According to Erika Cheetham, Nostradamus used techniques similar to those of the fourth Century neo-Platonist Iamblicus, whose book *De Mysteriis Egyptorum* he could easily have known and possessed, as it was reprinted at Lyons in 1547. Gazing into a bowl filled with water was like using a crystal ball, a way of obtaining a deep trance through meditation. Other procedures indicate that he used magical incantations and rituals to obtain his visions by becoming possessed by the spirits of the void, which appeared and dictated prophecies to him. It is clear that he was simultaneously inspired and terrified by the gods of prophecy.

The process was a meditation (or 'creative visualization', as it would now be called). Meditative procedures such as crystal gazing create a magical atmosphere that diminishes the control of the conscious mind, and contacts the processes of the inner unconscious and allows its contents to be withdrawn. Since it is widely acknowledged in modern psychology that our personal unconscious is connected to a collective unconscious, common to all humanity, it is possible that by utilizing such techniques to enhance his meditative faculties, Nostradamus could have seen into the future.

His typical quatrains are quite general and obscure, and can be applied after the fact to many different events in the world. An example from *Century* II,91 follows:

A great fire will be seen as the sun rises
Noise and light extending far northward
Death and cries are heard within the globe
Death by iron, fire, famine awaiting them.[5]

This quatrain could apply to any war or major fire and their after-effects, but the commentator Leoni saw the coming of World War III in this quatrain, and Cheetham an attack on the USA or Russia (northern countries), bombed at sunrise and followed by a period of devastation.

Nostradamus wrote in a pot pourri of languages, and often used anagrams for proper names. Some of these have been identified as being accurate, such as 'Hister' referring to Adolf Hitler, 'Chiren' as Henri II (spelled as Henric) and 'Ripas' for Paris. He also refers often to the 'New City', which could easily be New York City. In *Century*

VIII,1 are the words 'PAU', 'NAY' and 'LORON' in upper case, which while they are all small towns in western France, are also an anagram in French for 'NAPAULON ROY' — Napoleon the King.

Nostradamus was a spiritual and moral man who felt a great responsibility for the ramifications of his predictions. He believed that it was often necessary to pass over or obscure matters which could injure people, cities or nations, both in his own time and in future times. He also made the astute observation that kingdoms, sects and religions pass through stages of development, often at variance with their initial principles or their current leaders. These ideas implied that he had a highly developed philosophy about change in history and the future, and about the nature of time itself.

He knew that the act of prophecy was often tainted by suggestions of magic, particularly black magic, but he continually expressed his faith in the divinity of God and the inviolability of God's understanding of the nature of things.

Nostradamus was careful to exempt judicial astrology from negative connotations. Judicial astrology is the forecasting of events which will come to pass and conditions which will prevail, and is based on the horoscopes of countries, their royalty or rulers, and other agencies. Nostradamus used these techniques:

> by the aid of this [judicial astrology] it is, and by divine revelation and inspiration, united with deep calculations, we have reduced our prophecies to writing.'[6]

This form of astrology enables events to be dated far into the distant future.

Nostradamus' comments on the methods by which it is possible to understand things in the future refer to books which had come to him and writings which had lain hidden for many generations. He had read and was influenced by potent, magical texts, but decided ultimately to burn them, presenting them 'to Vulcan'. He reported that they burned with 'an unaccustomed brightness', creating a 'subtle illumination' over him and his house which acted as a catalyst for further divination and prophecy.

Celestial judgment (astrology) allowed him to harmonize his imagination with celestial figures. He stated that within his hallowed prophetic space, the three aspects of time (past, present and future) were clasped in one eternity. Nostradamus' ideas about time correspond to those of modern physicists and scientists such as Einstein and J. M. Dunne, that all pasts and futures exist within an eternal present. But Nostradamus contradicted the seeming inviolability of world events by stating that the free will exhibited by humanity made prediction difficult.

The Astrological *Centuries*

> . . . the things that are to happen can be foretold by nocturnal and celestial lights (the stars and planets), which are natural, coupled to a spirit of prophecy . . . amid prolonged calculation . . . I have composed books of prophecies, containing each one hundred astronomic quatrains of forecasts . . . from now to the year 3797.[7]

While Nostradamus describes his psychic, meditative and prophetic methods in the *Centuries*, he also used astrology to date many of his quatrains, often referring to constellations, planets and signs.

In the Preface to the first volume of *Centuries*, Nostradamus wrote a long explanatory letter to his son Caesar, in which he described that a '. . . Divine Being has permitted me to learn from the revolution of the stars.'[8] He referred to his inherited gift of occult prediction, which would remain confined to himself rather than being passed on to Caesar, but went on to state:

> . . . considering that the events of human proposal are uncertain, whilst all is governed and directed by the incalculable power of Heaven, guiding us, not by Bacchic fury, nor yet by Lympathic motion, but by astronomical assertion — Such alone as are inspired by the divine power can predict particular events in a spirit of prophecy.

He implied that while future events and their dates are determined by planetary movements in the heavens, their description remains to be modified by the spirit of prophecy. He considered astrology an 'unaided natural knowledge' which was capable of deciphering few of the secrets of the Creator on its own. He said that in past times

practitioners of Judicial Astrology had such power and impressions of
the future as to become inspired and prophetic. Indeed he says, 'He
who is called prophet now, once was called seer.'[9]

Most commentators misinterpret the astrological quatrains of
Nostradamus. For example, in Cheetham's *Prophecies of Nostradamus,*
in *Century* I,50, 'the three water signs' are described as being Aries,
Cancer and Aquarius, when only Cancer is a water sign. A close study
of the astrological quatrains, the methods of Nostradamus and the
interpretations of modern commentators yields a very interesting
picture.

The astrological quatrains are instructive because they show how
Nostradamus hinted at the timings of events in a subtle and hidden
way, only discernable by competent astrologers. Few of the quatrains
can be dated precisely by their astrological information, because they
describe planetary cycles or combinations which occur cyclically. The
astrological information must be cross-referenced with other names
and descriptive material within the quatrain to obtain a correct
interpretation. In this way, he was able to create a cyclical fabric of
times upon which to project astrologically and psychically as far into
the future as he liked.

Many of the quatrains are ambiguous, even with a sufficient
knowledge of astrology. In any given historical time it would have
been natural to assume the most recent manifestation of any astrological event as being the time referred to in the prophecy. This principle
may account for the phenomenal relevance of the prophecies to the
succession of different generations. Indeed, the quatrains themselves
often provide the most valuable clues to their own interpretation.

Because he created almanacs, Nostradamus was skilled at calculat-
ing planetary tables which projected astrological positions well into
the future. While he refers in the Introduction to the *Centuries* to the
year 3797, it otherwise appears that he limited his prophecies to the
year 2000. He thus restricted his predictions to the Age of Pisces, from
his own lifetime to AD 2000.

It is intriguing that although Nostradamus claimed to know the
dates of all of the *Centuries*, there are only five quatrains in the entire
work which have actual dates: III,77; VI,2 and 97; VIII,71; and X,72.

As an example of the possible duality in even the most specific
astrological quatrains, Cheetham suggested that *Century* I,50, entitled

'Third Antichrist?', indicated a person with three water signs who brings trouble to countries in the East. This is quite intriguing because Saddam Hussein of Iraq has a planetary grand trine in water signs of the three planets associated with destruction, Mars in Scorpio, Saturn in Pisces and Pluto in Cancer. But Kaiser Wilhelm of Germany also had the Ascendant in Cancer, Mars and Neptune in Pisces and the Moon in Scorpio, also in grand trine. Both of these men fit this qualification, and there are certainly more individuals in history who do likewise.

Century I,51 describes a conjunction of Jupiter and Saturn in the head of Aries. While this is most commonly interpreted as a conjunction of the two planets Jupiter and Saturn in Aries, it is incorrectly suggested by Cheetham and Wöllner that the next time it will happen will be in September 1995, and by Norab in September 1994, none of which is accurate. Throughout that period of time Saturn is in the sign Pisces, and Jupiter in either Scorpio or Sagittarius. In addition, it is probable that what Nostradamus meant by 'Chef d'Aries' was the constellation of the 'Head of the Ram', which contains the fixed star Alpha Arietis and was in the last degree of Aries in Nostradamus' time. There have been no conjunctions of Jupiter and Saturn on that degree since, although in 1821 there was such a conjunction at 24° Aries. Nostradamus therefore did not mean an event happening in our time.

Century I,16 mentions 'a scythe joined with a pond in Sagittarius'. Cheetham interprets this as Saturn and Aquarius in conjunction, which is impossible as Saturn is a planet and Aquarius is a zodiac sign, but it could mean Saturn (scythe) and the Moon (pond) conjunct in Sagittarius, which happens many times every $29\frac{1}{2}$ years when Saturn returns to Sagittarius and is conjoined by the Moon every month. The commentator Wöllner saw the year 1699, while Roberts saw 1999. This is an example of a quatrain which refers to a generic event which will happen periodically.

This raises an important point. The essential idea of astrology is that planetary aspect combinations describe events which happen in similar form every time the aspect recurs, although subsequent combinations of such configurations recur in different signs which modify the event. In Nostradamus' time only the planets from the Sun through Saturn were known. Within the limitation of Saturn's $29\frac{1}{2}$ year cycle, most planetary configurations with two, three or even four planets recur regularly, often many times each century. Conjunctions between Jupiter and Saturn, the two slowest of the classical planets, happen every twenty years, which seem to indicate successful or unsuccessful assassination attempts or the deaths of American Presidents elected in such years since 1860. It has happened with Presidents elected in 1860 (Lincoln assassinated), 1880 (Garfield assassinated), 1900 (McKinley assassinated), 1920 (Wilson died), 1940 (Roosevelt died), 1960 (Kennedy assassinated) and 1980 (attempted assassination of Reagan).

With the discovery of the outer planets, Uranus, Neptune and Pluto, the maximum cycle of the known planets has expanded almost to infinity. Uranus was discovered in 1781 by William Herschel, Neptune by Le Verrier and Galle in 1846, and Pluto by Percival Lowell in 1930. As the cycle of Uranus is 84 years, Neptune 165 years and Pluto 265 years, historical repetitions involving all outer planets happen very rarely. The dynamic of the recurrence of planetary configurations has therefore changed since Nostradamus' time.

In the last-mentioned quatrain the Saturn-Moon conjunction in Aquarius is very common because Saturn passes through each sign for $2^{1}/_{2}$ years every $29^{1}/_{2}$ years, and the Moon would pass Saturn every month throughout the cycle, approximately thirty times! When the realities of astrological cycles are understood in this way, some of Nostradamus' prophecies are bound to be correlated with more than one event because they happen so many times in every age. But the paradox is that most interpreters mistake them as referring to an event unique to their own time.

Even what look like very specific astrological configurations in Nostradamus often recur. *Century* II,48 states that 'The great army will pass over the mountains when Saturn is in Sagittarius and Mars moving into Pisces.'[10] Many commentators have suggested that this conjunction is rare and has only occurred once since publication, in July 1751, and Leoni predicts the next time will be the year AD 2193. In reality this is a common configuration and has happened three times already this century, in May 1928, November 1956 and November 1986.

In *Century* IV,67 Cheetham correctly states that the Saturn and Mars conjunction happens regularly. In fact it occurs ten times in the twentieth century, the last time in 1998. The quatrain seems to indicate a famine caused by excess heat, a meteor causing widespread damage, and a great place burning from hidden fires, possibly from wars or raids. While this is a recurrent configuration, it could also be extremely relevant to the destruction of the ozone layer, the famines which are increasing year by year, and the wars and strife which result from these conditions which will worsen in the future.

In *Century* VI,24, a conjunction of Mars and the sceptre, Jupiter, in the sign Cancer indicates a dreadful war after which a new king will be appointed. According to Wöllner it is a unique astrological event which will next happen on 21 June 2002, whilst it has already happened six times since 1812.

Century X,67 describes a very complex astrological time when in the month of May, Saturn is in Capricorn, Jupiter and Mercury are in Taurus, Venus is in Cancer and Mars in Virgo. Although all the quatrain describes is a fall of hail and possible earthquakes, it is very interesting in its astrological configuration. Suggested dates include 10 May of an unknown year or April 1929, which is wrong, while Wöllner suggests May 3755.

Astrological references in other quatrains are quite obscure or difficult to understand accurately. In *Century* VI,35 Nostradamus mentions an astrological event:

Near the Bear and close to the white wool,
Aries, Taurus, Cancer, Leo, Virgo, Mars, Jupiter;
the Sun will burn the great plain, woods and cities;
letters hidden in the candle.

The Bear is the constellation Ursa Major or Ursa Minor and the white wool could be the Milky Way, but otherwise it is impossible to decipher.

Fixed stars have been used by astrologers since ancient times in prediction and prophecy. Each of the important stars and constellations, in addition to those composing the zodiac, had their own significance and ruling planet. Thus stars ruled by Mars indicated warfare, danger from fire, anger, and other related martial qualities.

An example of a quatrain which uses fixed stars is *Century* VIII,90:

In a holy place (a crusader) will see a horned ox,
though the virgin pig's place will be satisfied,
order will no longer be sustained by the king.

The star Aldebaran (attributed to Mars) is the central star in the Horns of the Bull constellation, which traditionally indicates danger through poison, so this could be an accurate constellation.

Nostradamus himself questioned the level of quality of other astrologers. *Century* VI,100 is an incantation against inept critics and sub-standard astrologers, where Nostradamus rails against the ignorant herd, and chastises all those astrologers who have studied the subject insufficiently.

Alchemical and Kabbalistic Influences

Nostradamus was interested in alchemy, as were many of the most intelligent and perceptive men of his time, up to and including Isaac Newton. Alchemy evokes mysterious and magical images, and was a primary factor in the world view of Nostradamus.

In this century alchemy has become highly valued since the depth psychologist Carl Gustav Jung demonstrated that it is an early form of psychology. The art of making gold from base metals was the outer form of alchemy which obscured the inner form of the 'work', which was to transmute the base elements of the personality to a higher spiritual or transcendent reality. Many of the *Centuries* refer not to predictions, but to alchemical processes in which Nostradamus was interested.

A sample of his alchemical quatrains is *Century* II,2 where:

The divine word will give substance to heaven and earth, occult gold in a mystic deed. Body, soul and spirit are all powerful. Everything is beneath his feet, as at the seat of heaven.

Nostradamus implied that he used a Kabbalistic method of projection in addition to his divinatory, astrological and meditative practices. Many quatrains contain Kabbalistic concepts, such as references to firmaments and their spheres. Nostradamus discovered how to harness the angelic spirits resident in such places, and combined them with his astrological understanding to make prophecies about the Millennium.

The End of the World

Although Nostradamus mentioned the year 3797[11], he also described a series of events which point to cataclysms approaching the Millennium year 2000. As in the book of *Revelation* in the Bible, he foresaw that:

> . . . the sword of death is on its way to us now, in the shape of pestilence, war (more horrible than has been known for three generations of men), and famine, that shall fall upon the earth, and return to it at frequent intervals.[12]

Such an abundance of rain and fire will come that scarcely anything will remain unconsumed, but this precedes what Nostradamus called 'the Last Conflagration', which occurs when Mars completes its cycle. What he meant is unclear because he is obviously referring to his own system of planetary cycles, which is Kabbalistic in origin. He followed by stating that:

> . . . some will gather in Aquarius through several years, and others in Cancer, which will be of still longer duration.

He anticipated that many years after his time pestilence, famine and natural catastrophes would diminish the world, and that there would not be enough people to attend to agriculture. In support of this prophecy, during the coming eclipse of 1999, the powerful outer planets Uranus and Neptune, which indicate just such events, will be close to conjunction in the sign of Aquarius, after having been exactly conjunct throughout 1993 in the sign Capricorn.

The Millennium Cycle and the Prophecies

> When the Wheel of Time shall have come to the Seventh
> Millennium, there will begin the games of Death.
>
> from *Century* X, 74[13]

In the *Epistle to Henry II*, Nostradamus stated that his 'astronomic calculus' allowed him to project as far forward into the future as

historians (in his time) knew of the past. As he projected back to the
Creation six thousand years earlier, he was thus claiming to project
this far into the future.

Nostradamus referred to seven millennial periods in his epistles,
corresponding to the Hebrew Jubilee Year, and it is clear that he
described and dated predictions within these large units of time.
Century I,48 refers to the Jubilee Year cycle by saying that the Earth
would be destroyed before the Sun takes up its final cycle. In *Century*
X,74 he describes a year of the seventh number, implying the end of
the seventh Millennium around the year 2000. He went on to
prophesy games of slaughter not far from the time when the dead
would be reborn as mentioned in the books of *Revelation* and *Enoch*.
In *Century* III,79 the fatal and eternal order is invoked as turning on
its course, which also refers to the Millennium cycle.

It appears that in stating that the world would finally in the year AD
3797, as he wrote in the *Centuries*, he may have been using the 7000
years of seven millennia as the duration of the world, and subtracting
them to reconcile with an unorthodox Creation date of 3203 BC (3797
+ 3203 = 7000 years) to arrive at the 'End of the World'.

Nostradamus also used an unusual method to describe sub-cycles
of the world age. While their beginning and ending times are
ambiguous, the Moon would finish its cycle in the year 2250, having
begun in 1889. In the following Age of Saturn the celestial signs would
rule as the world nears its final death. He here referred to the
precessional ages and the coming Age of Aquarius.

Nostradamus described a tragic series of events, without parallel in
history, leading up to the Millennium in the year 2000. While many
of these overlap, the categories of major events approaching the
Millennium are the following:

- The Gulf War
- The Russian-US Prophecies
- The Three and the Commonwealth of Independent States
- England and the European Community
- The Papacy
- The Third Antichrist
- Incidents Towards the Millennium
- Natural Catastrophes

Nostradamus prophesied that political and religious changes would happen against a backdrop of natural catastrophes in the last years of the twentieth century. It is not exactly clear if he connected politics and religion together as cause and effect, but they certainly weave in and out of one another. It is this parallel which is frighteningly similar to contemporary events as we approach the Millennium year, because it is the combination of political disintegration aided by religious fundamentalism and ecological imbalance which is shaping the future world throughout the 1990s.

The Gulf War

Early 1991
Nostradamus describes a great war towards the Millennium involving 1991 bombings in the Middle East, a prophecy which eerily evokes the long war between Iran and Iraq, and Operation Desert Storm in 1991. *Century* VIII,70 describes a wicked and unpleasant tyrant terrorizing Mesopotamia. This is surely a reference to Saddam Hussein and the Gulf War, the 'dreadful and black land' being the burning of the oil wells in Kuwait by the Iraqis after their loss in Operation Desert Storm.

    Century V,23 is often attributed to the quatrains about the two allies, the US and the USSR, brought together through disarmament treaties. The allusion to Mars as the reason for the alliance could refer to the nuclear non-proliferation treaty, while a terrorized African leader could relate to Qaddafi of Libya. The prophecy that the 'Duumvirat' (twin alliance) would be shattered by a fleet could refer to the naval blockade which Iraq broke to start the Gulf War in early 1991.

Late 1993
Century IV,95 mentions a period of three years and seven months 1993 passing before a war occurs. This could refer to a war after an alliance between America and Russia. Cheetham suggests that a line in the quatrain which refers to 'two vestals' could be a corruption of 'vassals', or two smaller countries. This could refer to the events which followed the collapse of the USSR, and the two vassals could be smaller republics which still retain nuclear missiles and which are not included in the US-USSR alliance. As this friendly relationship began in 1990, it could presage a war in late 1993.

In *Century* III,95 Islamic law fails, but is followed by another less pleasing form of law. It also mentions a Russian river, the Dnieper, having to give way through tongues. This may be a breakdown of peaceful efforts to resolve Russian problems and the possibility of battles over control in the former USSR, or even problems with nuclear reactors in the former USSR. Already the Islamic republics along the southern boundary of the former USSR are bickering and threatening to form alliances with fundamentalist Islamic states to the south which are antagonistic to the West and to Russia.

Nostradamus suggests that armed forces arising from Armenia would come towards Europe. This prophecy echoes the liberation movements in the southern Russian republics of Armenia and Azerbaijan, which gained impetus in 1991, when they were given the opportunity to become independent after the collapse of the USSR. Furthermore, additional territorial disputes such as those in Nagorno-Karabakh have also been activated by former injustices.

There is an ever-present danger that nuclear weapons, formerly under the control of the USSR central government, will be claimed by newly-independent Soviet republics such as Azerbaijan, the Ukraine and others, as they break away and form separate republics.

The Russian-US Prophecies

Late 1980s

1980s   *Century* IV, 32 describes 'things held in common', a possible reference to Communism. The quatrain says that meat will give way to fish, implying a lowering of the standards of living, and that the old order (the Communist Party) will at first put up strong resistance, but once put down will very quickly disappear and lose influence. This has indeed happened in an astonishingly short time period.

1990-2005

1990s   In *Century* VI,21, there is mention of an alliance between the USSR and the US in the early 1990s, when the new man elected, Yeltsin, is supported by the Great One, either Gorbachev or the American President Bush. The quatrain also pictures a northern world racked by plagues, a possible reference to the AIDS epidemic of the last decade of this century.

In *Century* IV,50, Libra will be seen to reign in the West and no one will notice the strength of Asia destroyed until Seven hold the hierarchy in succession. While the Seven could be the group of seven most powerful nations which determine worldwide financial values, it is more likely to refer to the newly independent republics following the breakdown of the USSR in 1991. The individual republics declared independence and began negotiating with each other whilst vying for importance within the resultant Commonwealth of Independent States, consisting of the most powerful republics. This has aroused fear within the European Community, the US and abroad because of the tension between the republics due to disputes over army personnel and weapons and, in particular the disposal of the arsenal of nuclear weapons.

According to *Century* V,78, the US-USSR alliance will survive for no longer than thirteen years, when it will be forced apart by superior barbarian powers. There is a reference to a barque or ship, which could refer to the Papacy, but which could also mean the renamed St Petersburg, St Peter being the ship of the Church. Many of the Russian quatrains and others mention fallen leaders, which would apply to the large scale rejection of Lenin and other leading Communists after the collapse of the USSR in 1991.

Nostradamus notes that this period will usher in a return to power of the Church:

> The great Vicar shall be put back to his pristine state, but that desolated and abandoned by all, will return to the sanctuary destroyed by Paganism.[14]

As the Communists forcibly suppressed Christianity during their seventy-four-year reign, this prophecy could be very appropriate as the northern republics are now recreating their strong Christian belief as they become independent of the rule of the Communist Party and the USSR.

The group of Russian prophecies (including the above) refer to the 'Reds', the 'sickle', the 'Emperor of the North' or the 'Russian antipope'. In his *Epistle* to his son, Nostradamus described a series of events which are happening at the present time. He referred to worldwide famine and natural catastrophes related to climatic changes not unlike those projected as a result of the greenhouse effect and the dissolution of the ozone layer along with the 'Third King of the North', who he assumed to be either Russian or German. Upon receiving complaints from the people, the King will pass limits set by his forebears and will replace almost everything in its old condition.[15] The phrase 'Third King of the North' is intriguing because it could be inferred that the Czars were the first kings, the leaders of Communist regime from Lenin and Stalin to the dissolution of the USSR in 1991 the second kings, and the third king could signify the man (or men) to arise following the dissolution of the USSR. An even more incredible but feasible possibility is a return to monarchy.

The Three and the Commonwealth of Independent States

A key phrase which appears in a series of quatrains is the reference to the three brothers or 'the three'. This has often been correlated with the Kennedy brothers, particularly by Cheetham, but there is a possible alternative translation. The three could refer to the three former USSR republics of Russia, the Ukraine and Byelorussia, which formed the nucleus of the Commonwealth of Independent States in 1991. The prophecies then fit extremely well.

Early 1990s

1990-5   *Century* IX,36 shows the older king (Gorbachev) captured by the younger man (Yeltsin, by a few months), leading to a state of confusion. After being captives for a long time, the three (republics) will subsequently be wounded and murdered. This could indicate political and military pressure exerted after the ascendency of the core Commonwealth of Independent States by the other smaller republics.

    Century V,2 describes seven conspirators at a banquet rebelling and flashing their weapons 'against the three'. The quatrain also describes a leader being shot in the forehead through his armour. This could be a dangerous prediction of the less stable former USSR republics rebelling within the newly created Commonwealth of Independent States, forced by the seven major economic powers to rebel. The leader assassinated could therefore be either Yeltsin or the leader of one of the other republics. Gorbachev was forced out of government by New Year 1992, and Yeltsin will almost certainly follow him as a result of the early difficulties experienced by the people of the new Commonwealth due to starvation and economic chaos.

Sects unite against the red ones in *Century* IX,51, a clear reference to the rebellion of the republics formerly within the USSR and their declarations of independence in 1991 and 1992. It predicts that poverty and starvation will afflict all the republics but one, which will ruin the world. When the Commonwealth of Independent States was formed, some of the smaller republics retained part of the USSR nuclear arsenal, and Western analysts remain worried that these poor and disaffected republics could be easy prey for the Chinese or Islamic fundamentalist countries wanting to buy their weapons.

Three beautiful children mentioned in *Century* VIII,97, are born near a bank, but bring ruin to the people when they come of age. This could refer to the three republics forming the core of the Commonwealth of Independent States which, when they develop politically and militarily, become a threat to all those around them. It is these three republics which have retained most of the Soviet nuclear arsenal, military forces and naval fleet, and are considered a danger because of their unstable politics. Alternatively, the three beautiful children could also be the sons of Queen Elizabeth II, and their fated role the end of monarchy in England.

The 'two great leaders' of *Century* II, 89 'will be friends', their power will grow and the new land will be at the height of its powers. However, this allusion to the new alliance between America and Russia signals the emergence of the 'man of blood' and Nostradamus mentions that the alliance will last only three years and seven months. Cheetham thought that this referred to a potential coup in Russia, which did occur in August 1991, but it also seems to apply to the future of the temporary alliance between the individual republics of the former USSR. The old-guard Communist influence within the former USSR retains the threat of a coup d'etat. The man of blood may be a unifying politician who links together the most powerful republics of Russia and the Ukraine, and emerges as a brutal leader, or a spiritual leader who excites and agitates the masses to rebel in the 1990s.

1992

Three brothers put the world in trouble in *Century* VIII,17, but their enemies will seize the port city. Roberts sees this as a reference to a 199.

future world revolution. The 'brothers' are often taken to be the Kennedys, but could also refer to the three republics making up the new Commonwealth which succeeds the USSR, one of whose initial problems involves the ownership and control of the Russian fleet based in Black Sea ports. Hunger, fire, blood and plagues all amplify evil ways, and are the surest ways of producing violence and increasing the risk of military takeovers.

England and the European Community

Late 1970s
1970s   In *Century* VIII,87 a tall, thin and dry valet is seized whilst escaping from danger with sharp poison and letters in his collar. This is an obvious reference to Sir Anthony Blunt, Queen Elizabeth II of England's advisor on paintings who was discovered to be a Russian spy in the late 1970s. He was dismissed and severely reprimanded.

1990s
1990s   The 'things held in common among friends' in *Century* IV,32 is understood by Larmor as the fall of or problems with Communism, which was declining rapidly throughout the 1980s. Cheetham predicted in 1980 that this would mean a US-USSR alliance, which has now come about following the failure of Communism in the USSR and eastern Europe. It could also refer to the issues to be raised by the European Community during its controversial approach to monetary union in 1999.

The lady in an adulterous rage is described in *Century* VI,59. She conspires against her prince, which sounds suspiciously like the overthrown Margaret Thatcher becoming a conspirator against Prime Minister John Major. Following this, many pro-Thatcher Tories in Britain felt that they had been martyred. However, this prophecy could also be a reference to the British Euro-MPs feeling disenfranchised by John Major's reluctance to engage in full membership of the European Economic Community.

Similarly, *Century* VI, 74 suggests that she who was cast out will return to reign and punish her enemies in the process. There is also a mention of a critical event at the age of seventy-three years old in connection with a woman.

Late 1990s

Even prophecies previously attributed to other times can apply to   1995+
current affairs in the 1990s. *Century* V,51 describes people from the
Balkans, England, Poland and Czechoslovakia making a new alliance
to keep the Straits of Gibraltar open, while the Spaniards and Italians
hatch a cruel plot. Laver[16] attributed this to Second World War
alliances, but they could equally apply to the last years of this century.
The increasing strength of the European Community and its intention
to absorb eastern European countries such as the Balkan republics,
Poland and Czechoslovakia, could be an attempt to keep Gibraltar
open, in the sense that it opens all Europe as a united trading power.
Spain and Italy will be treated unfairly along the way. In *Century* V,35
the British Navy will arrive under cover of weather to conquer a city
with a stone in its stomach — a possible reference to the loss and
eventual recapture of Gibraltar, called 'the Rock'.

After 1999

In *Century* X,26 the 'successor', Prince Charles, will avenge his hand-   1999+
some brother, implying a catastrophe happening to Prince Edward or
the Duke of York. The quatrain then suggests that the death was an
obstacle and goes on to mention a long alliance between England and
France. By this time Prince Charles will have succeeded his mother,
Queen Elizabeth II, and will occupy the throne under the shadow of
vengeance. Could this imply that the Queen and her sons are to be
killed, or metaphorically that the monarchy is to be eliminated within
the European Community?

The Papacy

1980s

Scandals in sacred temples in *Century* VI,9 are thought of as honoured   1980s
and praiseworthy, although strange torments will be in store for the
conspirators concerned. This sounds very much like the Bank
Ambrosiana and Masonic scandals involving the Papal bank which
led to the brutal deaths of many of those involved.

1990s

The rapid advancement of five popes in twenty years towards the end   199 of the Millennium is described in *Century* V,92. The last pope, possibly the one following Pope John Paul II, will be unloved by the Romans (the other Cardinals?). *Century* V,46 describes Cardinals being internally divided and Rome being injured by Albanians. As Albania has only recently been free of oppressive Communist dictatorship since 1991, this could herald a rebellion that spreads into Italy, or a time when a contentious new pope is elected from this small country.

Century V,53 refers to the ascent of Christianity and suggests a millennial return to the law when the Grand Messiah returns in the Age of the Sun, that is, the twentieth century.

The Third Antichrist

Nostradamus refers in many of his *Centuries* to the 'Third Antichrist'. Many commentators think that Napoleon and Hitler were the first two Antichrists, and that the reign of the third Antichrist will originate in Russia in the last years of the 1990s. *Century* V,96 refers either to the 'Third Antichrist' or to 'The Three' being killed by the Antichrist. It could also therefore be a reference to the three initial republics making a coalition following the breakdown of the USSR in the early 1990s, and being responsible in some way for creating conditions for the arrival of the Antichrist.

1990s

1990s In *Century* V, 54 the Antichrist comes from beyond the Black Sea and 'Grand Tartary', (China), and the bloody rod he carries through southern Russia could be a metaphor for the collapse of and violence between the southern republics of the USSR in the 1990s. *Century* VI,33 is an anagram or cryptic version of the Antichrist — ALUS is suggested.

Late 1990s

1995+ *Century* VI,80 describes an Arabian kingdom stretching out to Europe, resulting in violence and driving the cross out to death. This may mean an explosive Middle Eastern war or the Islamic southern USSR republics revolting and spreading their influence towards Europe. There will certainly be a refugee problem in Europe throughout the 1990s because of the political instability in Eastern Europe and Russia.

Century V,62 refers to blood raining down on the rocks. The Sun is in the East and Saturn in the West. This is understood by Leoni to mean the opposition between Christianity and the Antichrist, while others interpret it as an East-West war in the closing years of this century. *Century* VIII,59 describes how the Eastern powers, twice cast down by the West, will return and win after many battles. Cheetham relates this to the Eastern Antichrist and his attempts to overthrow Western powers.

The Third Antichrist annihilates three brothers in *Century* VIII,77, after which there are twenty-seven years of bloody war. Water and a red hail will cover the surface of the Earth. This could be a war lasting through the first quarter of the twenty-first century.

In the *Preface* to his son, Nostradamus describes in detail the events leading up to the Millennium. After the preceding developments, the third Antichrist will come to power as an infernal prince, subsequently waging wars and fighting battles which will lead to burning towns and cities. After the rise to power of the Antichrist, he will place an 'antipope' on the throne of Rome and proclaim a new Holy Roman Empire, which will last only seven months, after which both will be killed and their supporters slaughtered. Children will be dashed and evils committed by Satan. After this has been endured for an unspecified period of time, there will be a reign of Saturn, an Age of Gold, when Satan will be diminished and powerless for one thousand years.

According to one commentator, P. Innocent Rissault, the Antichrist would start his career around 1980. With the final schism of the Roman Catholic church and the destruction of Rome in the year 2000, the Antichrist will be accepted as a Universal Monarch.

2000-2010

A rose appears upon the middle of the world in *Century* V,96, which   2000+
could be a reference to the Rosicrucian and Masonic symbol for Christ, but because the Christ energy will be responsible for new deeds, blood will be shed. The Awaited One will come too late, an interesting but disheartening reference to the Second Coming of Christ, anticipated at the Millennium itself. Maybe this implies that the delay is the result of the influence of the Antichrist.

Incidents Towards the Millennium

Nostradamus prophesied a trend which began gaining momentum and strength in late 1991 — the dissolution of the USSR leading to a rise in militant power and eventual aggression towards Europe. While it appears that he indicated military force and warfare, which is certainly happening now in many of the Middle Eastern and formerly communist countries, it could also refer to economic hardship and the destructive effect which the collapse of the Russian and Eastern European economies could have on the free world.

1980-90s

1980s Quatrain *Century* VIII,28 depicts such an inflation of paper money that it will amount to robbery ('milk being skimmed'), but they will all be thrown into the fire. This could be the scandals surrounding junk bonds, the bankruptcy of savings and loan banks in the US, the undermining of the credibility of Lloyds of London and the Japanese government in the 1980s and 1990s.

1991-2

1991-2 Among the events Nostradamus suggests is a complex Arab-Slavic invasion of Europe through Turkey and the Middle East. In *Century* IV,82 he mentions that masses of people coming from Slavonia (present day Yugoslavia) would sack their cities but would not extinguish the great flame, and indeed, throughout 1991-2, Serbian armies were at war with the other former Yugoslavian provinces, destroying many cities in what was formerly a united country. Yugoslavia broke apart just as the USSR did months earlier, but in an even more violent way. Old historical animosities were rekindled and there have been wanton killings between age-old rivals in adjoining territories. Similarly there is unrest and violence in Turkey, northern Iraq and many of the mainly Islamic republics of what was formerly the southern USSR.

In *Century* IV,82, masses of men come from Slavonia, ruining the Old City, with no one being able to extinguish the flames. This could refer to the breakdown of Yugoslavia and the war between the Serbs and Croatians, in which Dubrovnik and other cities were destroyed throughout 1991 and 1992.

Century VI,96 speaks of a great city abandoned to soldiers, creating a moral problem. This evokes the Serbian invasions of Croatia and Boznia throughout 1991, in which historical cities such as Dubrovnik were bombed and destroyed, forcing their inhabitants to flee, and leaving soldiers as their sole occupants. The frightening aspect of this conflict and its prediction is that Yugoslavia is so close to the centre of Europe.

1993
Century II,91 concerns 'the great star', possibly Halley's Comet in 1986. 1993
The quatrain suggests a date seven years later for the possible beginning of a Third World War.

Mid 1990s
Century III,97 describes the creation of a new land around Syria, 1994-8
Judea and Palestine. In the light of the Middle East peace negotiations in 1991-2, it could mean the creation of an independent Palestinian homeland in the coming years. The quatrain also mentions that the great barbarian empire will fall before the end of the century, which could refer to the USSR, Iraq, England or the USA.

In *Century* V,8 Nostradamus describes fire, hidden death and cities reduced to rubble. This could refer to new weapons of war, or to a great war as the Millennium approaches.

In *Century* VIII,41 a fox is elected by publicly playing the saint while privately feathering his nest, which could refer to almost any American politician and the nature of electoral politics in the US during the 1990s, particularly the Presidential election of 1992.

In *Century* VI,97, the 'sky burns at forty-five degrees', and widespread fires approach the New City, which has always been taken to represent New York City, which lies at 41 degrees north latitude. This could refer to the holes in the ozone layer which have opened over major population centres. In *Century* IX,92 the king will want to enter the New City to subdue it, but stays far away from the enemy. A captive speaks falsely. This could indicate American elections taking place during an apocalyptic millennial war during which the king (President) must remain away from New York. As recrimination and lying have become an integral part of American politics in recent years, this could accurately portray any critical election.

1999

1999   The 'three brothers' occur again in *Century* VIII,46 where the unrest
leads to millennial violence and increased bloodshed. This quatrain
refers to the shift of the Earth's axis in 1999. The American Eagle is also
mentioned, possibly a reference to the changed relationship to the US
and its interest in maintaining order in Russia. Or, the eagle may refer
to the incoming Age of Aquarius, of which it is symbolic.

Century X,72 is one of the most famous prophecies because it
mentions the year 1999 and seven months as the time when the Great
King of Terror will arrive, but Nostradamus also says that a time of
peace will follow. (see also pp. 105, 110-13.)

2000

2000   *Century* VI,10 is a millennial quatrain which contrasts black and
white, and red and yellow, thus implying racial divisions as the
primary cause of strife and bloodshed. Black and white often refer to
moral issues of evil versus good, while red and yellow may correspond to the Russians and Chinese who, when they have carried off
their possessions, bring blood, plagues, fire and hunger. This quatrain
is particularly interesting because the psychic Edgar Cayce described
exactly the same racial discrimination and anger as a cause of
bloodshed in the 1990s and beyond. The rioting in Los Angeles in
1992 is an example of the tension which is getting stronger in the US,
despite the erroneous perception that it is improving.

Century VI,98 combines the images of a great city tainted by
pestilence with a darkening of the Sun and Moon, a plundering of
wealth, the violation of temples and the reddening of two rivers. In
feeling it evokes a future apocalyptic New York, passed on both sides
by rivers, although intimations of this can be seen today. It also sounds
very much like the Biblical prophecy in the book of *Revelation*, and
may be keyed off by the powerful eclipse of mid-1999.

August 2000

According to *Century* V,25, a new Arabian Empire will attack Persia,
Egypt, Turkey and the Christian navies. While the commentator
McCann stated that the accompanying astrological configuration of
Sun, Venus and Mars conjunct in Leo will happen in August 1987, it
will also recur in the early days of August 2000.

2002

A conjunction between Mars and Jupiter in Cancer will usher in a 2002 calamitous war according to *Century* VI,24. Shortly afterwards, the new king will bring an extended peace. This could coincide with millennial expectations about the Second Coming, and corresponds to Nostradamus' projections of war followed by a long peace.

Natural and Environmental Catastrophes

1991

Those quatrains which refer to burning, hot winds, fires that cannot 1991 be put out, and other such metaphors may depict the depletion and elimination of vast areas of the ozone layer around the world. Holes already exist over northern Europe and Scandinavia, Australia and North America, as well as over the poles. *Centuries* I,16 and 17 describe droughts lasting forty months or years, followed by great floods, which are effects of the ozone hole cause. The first describes a time when Saturn is in Aquarius, as it is from February 1991 to January 1994, when a great war could be initiated as the century approaches its renewal.

1996

A Saturn and Mars conjunction is described in *Century* IV,67. The 1996 most likely date in the near future is 21 March 1996, when they are together in Pisces and the Sun is conjunct to Mars. The air is extremely dry, hidden fires make great places burn with heat, there is little rain, and droughts, hot winds and wars. Such terrible famines and natural disasters are the result of an increase of heat — certainly a reference to the quickly deteriorating ozone layer and the danger from drought and blinding ultraviolet rays.

Century VI,5 suggests a great famine caused by pestilence — a classic Biblical plague. This is particularly relevant because it will happen one hundred leagues from the hemisphere. It is currently being suggested that the increasing size of the hole in the ozone layer directly above the North and South Poles is responsible for climate changes which affect the entire food chain. Cattle and sheep in Australia, New Zealand and South America are going blind with cataracts caused by the ultraviolet rays from the sun without the ozone layer protection. The increasing temperature due to the greenhouse effect will alter weather patterns as well as the ecology of all lands. This is already leading to mass starvation, and the severity of the problem will increase in the future.

Century IX,88 states that when the Sun is in twenty degrees of Taurus there will be a great earthquake, where the theatre will be ruined. Prayers to both the faithless God and the Saints go unheeded. This could mean a major earthquake in California, because of its central role in the making of movies. There have been many earthquakes in Los Angeles and San Francisco in recent years, but the Sun passes twenty degrees Taurus every year about 10 April, so it cannot be dated more accurately. Also, in Spring 1992 the volcano at Mt Etna in Sicily erupted, endangering the nearby village and Taormina, which has a wonderful Greek amphitheatre.

Century IX,55 describes a dreadful war creating a pestilence the following year, when diseases will attack children and animals and few will survive it. Blood, fire and France are implicated, as well as Jupiter. Jupiter is the planet governing the blood, and France may be where the AIDS virus could become particularly virulent. This quatrain is quite alarming because of its augury of the murderous effect of the virus on humanity at large.

The overall effect of the *Centuries* is very powerful, and the range of the quatrains still to be attributed to events is vast. It is easy to see how they could have been successfully used to describe current and future events for more than five hundred years, for with every new reading of the complete quatrains it is possible to see allusions to recent and current events in the world.

Chapter Seven

Psychics, Seers and Mystics

Throughout history certain individuals have seen into the future. Their tools have varied, but most have felt a sense of being preordained to see ahead and a responsibility to guide other souls towards their own fulfilment. Inevitably these psychics, seers or mystics have made projections about the Millennium. We will consider some of the more notable of these.

During the Middle Ages many prophets and religious visionaries made millennial prophecies. The most famous of these were the medieval Saints Malachy, Hildegard, Bridget and Vincent, and the twelfth-century abbot Joachim of Fiore, all of whom predicted the end of the world. Their predictions were subsequently used to bully the faithless into joining the church.

Prophecies were often attributed to historical personages who could not deny their authenticity. Among the many such notable persons from whose writings such prophecies were extracted are the Venerable Bede, Edward the Confessor, Henry II of England, Thomas Beckett, Friar Roger Bacon, Geoffrey Chaucer, Ignatius Loyola, James I of England, Sir Walter Raleigh and Archbishop Ussher.[1]

The Papal Prophecies of Malachy

Malachy O'Morgair was born in the eleventh century. He was considered to be a holy man, having performed miracles, including healing the sick, levitating and making prophecies. When he died in 1184, while on a visit to St Bernard of Clairvaux, he left among his effects a series of short, enigmatic statements regarding the identity of the sequence of popes from his time until the end of the twentieth century. He was subsequently canonized as St Malachy.

The peculiar prophecies left by Malachy are mysterious and wonderfully apt descriptions of the popes. For example, Pope Alexander IV had been Cardinal of Ostia, and he was named *'Signum Ostiensis'*. The description of the nineteenth century Pope Leo XIII was *'Lumen in Caelo'* (Light in Heaven), extremely appropriate for a man whose family crest was a comet. Pope John XXIII, who had originally been Patriarch of Venice, was called *'Pastor et Nauta'* (Pastor of the Sea). Pope Paul VI, whose coat of arms carried the fleurs-de-lys, was called *'Flors Florum'* (Flower of Flowers). John Paul I, whose reign only lasted thirty-three days, was *'De Medietate Lunae'* (of the Half Moon), and he met his death in the middle of the lunar month, one month after taking office.

Some of the others include:

Alexander VII (1655-67)	*'Montium Custos'* (Guardian of the Hills)
Clement XIII (1758-69)	*'Rosa Umbriae'* (Rose of Umbria)
Clement XIV (1769-75)	*'Ursus Velox'* (Swift Bear)
Pius VI (1775-99)	*'Peregrinus Apostolicus'* (Apostolic wanderer)
Gregory XVI (1831-46)	*'De Balneis Etruriae'* (From the Baths of Etruria)

The present Pope John Paul II is *'De Labore Solis'* (Labour of the Sun) and, due to the waning popularity of Roman Catholicism, this could also be translated as 'from the Lonely Labour.' Malachy lists two more popes to follow the present John Paul II, *'Gloriae Olivae'*, and, lastly, *'Petrus Romanus'*, or 'Peter of Rome'. At that point, the Last Judgment will happen. Using Malachy's timing, it has always been assumed that the end of the papacy will occur around the Millennium year 2000, a date which agrees with Nostradamus.

Mother Shipton's Prophecies

Mother Shipton was a famous Yorkshire folk prophet who lived in a cave. The first recorded mention of her is in 1641, and her prophecies were published in one form or another more than twenty times between 1641 and 1700. Although long dead, her prophecies seemed to increase in number and accuracy from generation to generation, until they proliferated everywhere. She was thought to have prophesied the Great Fire of London and complex political changes throughout England.

One of her rhymes which spelled the end of the world was:

The world to an end will come,
In sixteen hundred and eighty-one.

As the preordained time approached, villagers throughout the north and west of England spent nights out in the fields confessing their numerous sins and crying for mercy, but the appointed time came and went. It turned out to have been a minor misreading of the corrupted text, and the revised, true version was:

The world will end we'll view
In sixteen hundred and eighty-two.

It is evident what happened — each year new prophecies were discovered which extended the true prophecy, until her influence simply lost all claim to the truth.

William Miller and the Millerites

William Miller, a New Englander, lived in the mid-nineteenth century. He was a highly religious man and a serious student of the Biblical prophets, especially Daniel. In Daniel's prophecies he saw that God had betrayed His secret: the world would end in 1843. This discovery forced him into immediate action, particularly because he had contemporaries who had their own rival proclamations, such as Harriet Livermore stating 1847, Joseph Woolf of Jerusalem, and Captain Saunders of Liverpool. Miller's calculations[2] were as follows:

Calculation I

From the rebuilding of Jerusalem, 457 BC, to the Crucifixion, 70 weeks of 7 years	490
From the crucifixion to paganism	475
From the Abomination of Papal Civil Rule	30
From the setting up to the end of above	1260
From the end of Papal Rule to the end of the World	45
Total	**2300**

Minus 70 'weeks' of seven years	490
Total	1810
Add the term of Christ's Life	33

| The End of the World | AD 1843 |

To Miller the proof was definite and irresistible. And, as if this was not enough for the sceptics, he confirmed it:

Calculation II

The House of Israel punished seven times for their sins;	
Leviticus xxvi., seven years of 360 days	2520
Subtract the date of the Babylonian Captivity (BC date)	677

| The End of the World | AD 1843 |

He also revealed the exact day — the vernal equinox on 21 March 1843. Within months his calculations had spawned a Pentecostal sect called the Millerites which spread rapidly. Many wild meetings were held and joyful expectation filled the followers.

A local businessman, Joshua V. Hines, figured, in the good old American tradition, that it would be easy to make a profit on a movement which was already very successful. He organized a campaign which was launched with the slogan: 'End of the World in '43'. He encouraged followers, preached to the unbelievers, and raised money for the furtherance of the message. Then came a comet which streaked across the skies, a sign to confirm the coming event, and thousands of people left Boston to move into the surrounding countryside, where many waited in white ascension-clothes. They came to watch the stars fall, but nothing happened.

The calculations had again been faulty, and the time was extended to encompass the end of the Hebrew Year, but when 31 December 1844 passed, and all the alternative dates had been exhausted, the Millerites disbanded with much weeping and gnashing of teeth. William Miller died broken-hearted.

Edgar Cayce — The Sleeping Prophet

Edgar Cayce was born on a small farm in the American state of Kentucky in 1877 and lived until 1945. Although he was poorly educated in the traditional sense, he developed a reputation for providing expert material derived from psychic trance sessions on a wide variety of subjects, present and future.

While Cayce was still a child he received the inner call to develop his clairvoyant powers. One day, while seven years old, he experienced a blinding light and a distinct message asking what he would most like to do with his life. As he had always been interested in helping sick children, he focused upon this manifestation. Shortly afterwards he was requested by the voices to sleep and that they would help him in whatever way they could. Over many years he became a famous channel of psychic material, mostly in sessions with individuals wishing to find out about their health and to discover ways of healing themselves.

While he made his living by running a photographer's shop in Virginia Beach, Virginia, he did health readings for an estimated 15,000 people. He would lie down on a couch, loosen his clothes to get comfortable, and then wait for the inner light which would signal connection with his channel. In his sessions he diagnosed illnesses of all varieties and prescribed remedies to cure them. He often described conditions and named treatments, remedies and drugs in terms known only to highly educated doctors. It was often necessary for his associates or patients to expend much effort tracking down the remedies and formulae detailed by Cayce while in his trances. And, because of the depth of his trances, he never remembered anything afterwards. One explanation he proposed was that he was able telepathically to enter the minds of doctors or scientists and thus understand their thought processes. This does not, however, do justice to his proven abilities.

He identified many strange conditions, often attributing them to inherited or reincarnational influences. He was able to diagnose people at a distance. It did not matter how far away his patients were, but he did have to know where they were while he was entranced. He regularly mentioned remedies or formulae for people who only contacted him at a later date.

He gradually discovered that he had a gift for precognition as well
as for healing. In the course of his medical work he also received and
made controversial predictions about the future. When he saw
flaming chariots rushing past his garden as a child, he foretold the
outbreak of war — the First World War.

His business advice was highly regarded and made many men rich.
Before his death he predicted a real estate boom in Virginia Beach,
where he spent most of his life, and indeed it increased its population
fifty times over! He predicted that the then sleepy town of 5000 people
would become a major East Coast port, which it now is. When he
advised businessmen about their investments during the early months
of 1929, he mentioned in the readings that the temporary fluctuations
signified a longer negative slide of all stocks and bonds for years to
come. He had predicted the Wall Street Crash months before it
happened!

Cayce and the Universal Mind

From the mid 1920s Cayce received and relayed prophetic messages
about individuals and the world. He dictated a wide range of
entranced lectures on a variety of subjects, in the belief that he was
a channel for information emanating from the group unconscious, or
what Jung called the 'collective unconscious'. Cayce's term for this
was the 'Akashic Record' or the 'Book of Life'. It is the:

> record that the individual entity writes upon the skein of Time and
> Space, through Patience, and opened when self has attuned to the
> Infinite, and may be read by those attuning to that consciousness.[3]

These records emanated from what he called the 'Universal Mind' and
he acknowledged that his role was as a channel for these energies.

In 1939 he predicted the deaths of two American presidents whilst
in office, relating them to themes of racial and labour strife, and the
violence of the country. These came to pass indirectly in the death of
Franklin Roosevelt in 1945 and directly in John F. Kennedy's
assassination in 1963.

Cayce predicted in 1937 that there was to be a 'new awakening' in
many portions of the Earth. And in 1943 he described the heralding

in of a new age, an Atomic, Space or Spiritual Age, beginning with the defeat of the Axis powers, and insisted that the actual timing was still God's concern.

The Fate of Nations

Edgar Cayce had radical ideas about how history would proceed from his time, and recognized a great need for revolutionary changes in the attitude of all humanity. He was correct in many ways, and may well be proven to be accurate in others.

One of his most unlikely predictions, which is suddenly beginning to seem possible, is that Russia would be 'born again'. Among his last prophecies, he saw the end of Communism in the USSR, and saw the hope of the world's religious development subsequently stemming from Russia. He also stated;

> But Freedom, freedom! That each man will live for his fellow man. The principle has been born there. It will take years for it to be crystallized. Yet out of Russia comes again the hope of the world.[4]

What was even more astonishing for the 1930s was that he believed the new Russia would ally itself with and be guided by the United States to achieve this position:

> By what will it [Russia] be guided? By friendship with that nation which hath even placed on its monetary unit 'In God We Trust'.[5]

While whatever religious revival there is in Russia at present is only in its early stages, this could be a powerful and accurate prophecy.

Whilst he saw China as the catalyst to the alliance between the US and Russia, he also saw the dramatic changes which are already evident in China. The Chinese people would increasingly lean toward Christianity and democracy, which would coincide with a consolidation of religious sects. The development would take time, moving like a stream through the land, while the country itself would ask to be left alone. Yet one day China would awake and become a cradle of Christianity as Russia had been.

He detailed the 'sins' of many countries which impeded true

planetary equality and enlightenment. The sin of America is not to act according to the principle of 'In God We Trust'. The sin of England is to espouse ideals of being better than other people, rather than growing to that which one deserves. The sin of France is an attachment to gratifying the desires of the body. The sin of Italy is to have abused Christian principles in the days of Rome. The sin of India is to be a cradle of knowledge not applied to the self. The sin of China is to want to be left alone in the world. Cayce prophesied coming events which would teach these countries their lessons.

While he did not know the timing of these events, he prophesied a series of dramatic social changes in the US towards the end of the century, including a revolution which would bring down the wealthy and raise up the poor and hungry, a 'levelling' of the rights of brother with brother, in racial terms as well. He saw a great internal repressive force coming from within the United States, which would take control of the country and proclaim its rights, but which would be economically and racially discriminative. He said that such a development was inevitable. The people's rights, particularly those of the poor and the homeless, were so thoroughly abused during the recent terms of Presidents Ronald Reagan and George Bush under the guise of equality, that it is leading America to revolutionary tension in the 1990s. These just grievances culminated in the murder and extensive rioting in Los Angeles in April 1992 in response to a court judgment which virtually everyone knew to be racist and unfair.

Cataclysms Approaching the Millennium

Cayce predicted a series of cataclysmic events happening over a sixty year span, leading up to the year 2000, but particularly from 1958 to 1998. In a reading given in 1934 he described these changes:

- The Earth will be broken up in the western portion of North America.
- The greater portion of Japan must go into the sea.
- The upper portion of Europe will be changed in the twinkling of an eye.
- Land will appear off the east coast of America.
- Open waters will appear in Greenland.

Figure 9. Edgar Cayce's World Map After the Inundation. According to Edgar Cayce, the dark areas will be lost under water after the inundations resulting from the shift of the Earth's axis around the year 2000.

- Upheavals in the Arctic and in the Antarctic will make volcanoes erupt in the torrid areas.
- Land will appear between Tierra del Fuego and Antarctica.
- A shifting of the poles — frigid or semi-tropical climates will become more tropical, and moss and ferns will grow.

These [changes] will begin in those periods in 1958 to 1998 when these will be proclaimed as the periods when His light will be seen again in the clouds.[6]

Cayce predicted destruction on a wide scale in Los Angeles, San Francisco and New York, intimating that it would happen towards the last ten years of the forty-year period he specified—from 1988 to 1998. In 1990 there was a gigantic earthquake in the area of south San Francisco which caused widespread destruction, and was followed in 1991 by a massive fire in the Oakland hills which destroyed thousands of homes and hundreds of acres of residential areas. He placed the destruction of Manhattan after the California cataclysm.

The damage prophesied in the United States towards the end of the 1990s includes inundations throughout the midwestern American states such as Mississippi, Missouri and Louisiana, and the subsequent emptying of the Great Lakes into the Gulf of Mexico. Many parts of the north-east coast, such as Connecticut and New York, will be severely disturbed. New York City itself will disappear, as will parts of South Carolina and Georgia.

Much of the flood damage Cayce predicted was to be caused by the shifting of the Earth's mantle, the hot layer beneath its surface upon which float the continents and land masses. He envisioned a drop of thirty or more feet, which would flood most lands on the planet. It is interesting that this phenomenon is happening at present because of the depletion of the ozone layer and global warming. These are both contributing to a melting of the Arctic and Antarctic ice mantles and subsequently raising the world's sea level. Once again, Cayce may have been right without understanding the precise cause of the inundations.

There will be an increase in volcanic rumblings in the western Pacific, which Cayce called the 'Ring of Fire', an arc encompassing Japan, China, south east Asia, Australasia and South America. He visualized Japan falling into the sea and disastrous changes throughout the area. It is known even now that Japan is indeed gradually falling into the sea.

Cayce predicted that Europe would be changed beyond recognition. Both polar regions would erupt and the poles shift position. Land would also be created off the eastern coast of the US, and cold climates such as northern Europe and England would become tropical. These dire predictions would be caused by an axis shift and the change of world ages. He saw a new cycle beginning at that time, heralded by geological shifts.

One of his favourite target areas was the Sicilian volcano, Mt Etna, which Cayce said would presage the tilting of the Earth's axis, particularly in the years after 1958. In the years since Cayce's predictions, Soviet scientists have determined that Etna has risen up to twenty-five feet higher than its last major eruption in 1960. While Etna has remained active, it was not until 1991 that it overflowed in a dangerous way, destroying Fornazzo, the village at its base, forcing thousands of people to move to safety. In early 1992 it erupted again, sending a massive lava flow towards a hill town on its slopes.

His readings link the eruptions of Mt Vesuvius in Italy and Mt Pelée in Martinique with a triggering off of volcanic activity all over the Earth. Cayce said that if Vesuvius or Pelée were to erupt, within three months this would provoke substantial activity in the southern coast of California, particularly the areas between Salt Lake City and southern Nevada, as well as in the southern hemisphere. Indeed, in Spring 1992 this is exactly what is happening, with a series of earthquakes measuring six on the Richter Scale in southern California. It is interesting that the very destructive Philippine eruptions of 1991 have affected the entire planet by their effect on the thinning of the ozone layer. It is predicted that the coming of more powerful volcanoes such as Mt Taal in the Philippines could drastically affect the entire ecology of the planet, as Cayce suggested.

Cayce determined that from 1968 to 1969 new land would appear in the Caribbean Sea, and according to geologists upheavals under water in that area have dramatically changed the ocean floor, if not creating new land in the way that Cayce projected. He believed that the present eastern seaboard of the US would be under water, but that new land would emerge from the ocean floor and eventually be habitable. He predicted that his home area of Virginia Beach would be among the few areas of safety, as would parts of Ohio, Illinois, Indiana and Canada.

Cayce and other psychics have predicted minor Earth disturbances in the time from 1980 to 1990, and major upheavals and worldwide catastrophic disasters from 1990 to 2000. It is almost as though the 1980s were a warming-up period for the devastation of the last decade of the Millennium.

The Biblical Cayce

Cayce was strongly influenced by the Bible, especially the books of *Daniel* and *Revelation*, and his prophecies were often phrased in language reminiscent of the Biblical prophets:

> These changes on Earth will come to pass, for the time and times and a half times are at an end, and there begin those periods for the readjustments. For how hath He given? The righteous shall inherit the Earth. Hast thou, my brethren, a heritage in the Earth?[7]

Cayce not only believed that Russia would become a spiritual centre in the New World after the earthquakes and axis change, but also that China would become the cradle of Christianity 'when it awoke'.

Cayce continually warned about the Coming of the Lord, and the approach of the day of reckoning, saying that the unfaithful must change or be condemned. He also stated that the 'day of the Lord is near at hand,' which is very like the Biblical prophets in tone, content and context. He saw the coming of the One, and that His Day would come on Earth. In this way Cayce was highly moralistic and fatalistic. He believed that the natural catastrophes towards the end of the 1958-98 period would foreshadow the Second Coming of Christ.

> And those [changes] will begin in those periods in '58 and '98, when these will be proclaimed as a period when His Light will be seen again in the clouds.[8]

When asked about the Second Coming of Christ, he answered;

When those that are His have made the way clear for Him. Don't think that there will not be trouble . . .⁹

Following the disruption of the world at the Millennium, the goal of humanity would be to reconstruct the New Jerusalem. Cayce saw this as a powerful symbol of renewal and rebirth.

To those then, that are come into the new life, the new understanding — the new regeneration, there *is* then the new Jerusalem — not as a place, alone, but as a condition, as an experience of the soul.¹⁰

The New Age had already begun in his time, and the New Jerusalem was present.

The Incarnations of Edgar Cayce

A positive light amidst Cayce's generally gloomy prophetic utterings is his belief in reincarnation. He knew he would return again, and his followers continually prodded him for information about who he would be in his next life, when it would be, and where it would be. He remembered his own previous incarnation in 1742 as a swash-buckling Cornish mercenary in the British Army prior to the American War of Independence.

He had landed in that life very near to where he lived as Edgar Cayce two centuries later. He saved a stockade of settlers at Fort Dearborn, near present-day Chicago, and Cayce believed that many of the people he encountered there had reincarnated again with him in this life, and that their previous life problems even became issues in their current lives. The idea of Group Karma — that whole groups of people reincarnate together throughout many historical ages — was a central belief of Cayce's.

Cayce also described another past life as Ra-Ta, an Egyptian priest. On a more optimistic note, he also predicted his return in another incarnation in 1998, as 'a possible liberator of the world'.¹¹ He often lapsed into other languages, some of which were recognizable while others were not, and yet he consciously knew no other language than English. This may imply other incarnations in different cultures.

After the particularly traumatic experience of being accused of practising medicine without a licence, he dreamt of being born again in Nebraska in AD 2100. At that time the sea covered the western part of North America, and his city was on the coast. When he declared himself to be the reincarnation of Edgar Cayce, two hundred years earlier, he was taken to be examined by a group of long-haired scientists. Together with these caricature scientists, Cayce travelled in a cigar-shaped flying ship to the locations of his earlier residences. From the air he saw the new and unfamiliar topography of the eastern US. Water covered parts of Alabama, while Norfolk, Virginia was a great seaport and New York City had been destroyed by an earthquake and was being rebuilt. Most houses were made of glass. Although some of Cayce's followers have been depressed at the thought of hundreds of years of catastrophes and natural disasters, Cayce himself was very optimistic about the future and had a vision that the power of God to influence humanity would have increased by that time. Certainly, it gives hope that a world will exist at that time.

Jung's *Seven Sermons to the Dead* [12]

In 1916[13] the psychologist Carl Jung had a vision which he felt compelled to write down. He subsequently found it so powerful that he had it privately published in a limited edition for friends and associates as *VII Sermones ad Mortuos*. Jung was investigating mysteries of the spirit and the unconscious, and had a particular interest in Gnostic thought, which his vision represented. He was Christian, but was also intrigued by all manifestations of the spiritual, such as comparative religion, mysticism, astrology, spiritualism and alchemy.

Although Jung was interested in the psychological aspects of these phenomena, he realized that the only way to truly understand them was to experience them himself. He considered Gnostic consciousness to be an archaic or source experience leading to the shadow world. Jung appreciated this avenue because he was a healer of souls, and as such understood the millennial experience which hypnotized the ancient mind.

Jung's visionary experiences were angelic and demonic in turn, and many of his visionary images were illustrated in his notebooks. They are particularly dramatic and controversial, which almost certainly explains why he kept them secret for so much of the early phase of his career. The sermons touch upon such subjects as creation, gods and devils, sexuality, man and woman, the church and the soul.

The language of the sermons is very much like the late Roman Gnostic texts studied by Jung, and the voices are prophetic. A portion of the seventh sermon reads like a biblical prophecy:

> At immeasurable distance standeth one single Star in the zenith.
>
> In this world is man Abraxas, the creator and the destroyer of his own world.
>
> This Star is the god and the goal of man.
>
> This is his one guiding god. In him goeth man to his rest. Toward him goeth the long journey of the soul after death. In him shineth forth as light all that man bringeth back from the greater world. To this one god man shall pray.
>
> Prayer increaseth the light of the Star. It casteth a bridge over death. It prepareth life for the smaller world and assuageth the hopeless desires of the greater.
>
> When the greater world waxeth cold, burneth the Star.
>
> Between man and his one god there standeth nothing, so long as man can turn away his eyes from the flaming spectacle of Abraxas.
>
> Man here, god there.
>
> Weakness and nothingness here, there eternally creative power.
>
> Here nothing but darkness and chilling moisture. There wholly sun.
>
> Whereupon the dead were silent and ascended like the smoke above the herdsman's fire, who through the night kept watch over his flock.[14]

Jung's vision showed him that the fiery force of the primeval union of opposites, symbolized by Abraxas, the part of our unconscious which has not yet attained consciousness, seeks to go beyond the material, sensual world. In a way this process requires the death of that material world before spiritual understanding can occur.

The metaphor carried in these verses is that our attitude towards the physical world must be allowed to die in order for our inner world and its guidance to be accepted and trusted. In this way Jung prepared himself for individual unification with God as a central principle of psychic wholeness. This is also a possible explanation for the universal need of millennial prophecies in all ages and within all religions. We need to go beyond the physical, material world in order to contact our higher, spiritual Self. And wholeness within ourselves is a prerequisite for wholeness in our world.

Modern Prophets of Doom

The Divine Plan of the Ages was written in 1886 by a Seventh Day Adventist, C. T. Russell, and attained a circulation of six million copies in a number of languages. He purported to show in this book that God is propelling us towards the end of the Millennium.

As we approach the time of doom we must remain aware of God's higher purpose and divine plan in creating the world as he has, and in the way it has been orchestrated. Russell felt that it was his purpose to bring the light of the sacred secret to the many. The apocalyptic ideas of Russell and other Christian prophets of doom are being carried on by the Watch Tower and Summit Lighthouse organizations today.

The 'messengers', Mark and Elizabeth Clare Prophet, claim to be in psychic contact with Jesus Christ and the Virgin Mary, the Buddha, Confucius, the Comte de St Germain, the Masters of the Himalayas and other ascended masters, all members of the Great White Brotherhood. Elizabeth Clare Prophet predicted, on the basis of the Cosmic Clock (a new age astrology for charting the cycles of karma and initiation given to them by the Mother Mary) that the world would be devastated in a cataclysm in 1990 and commanded her thousands of followers to sell all their property and move to a vast ranch in the Montana mountains. Needless to say, it did not happen.

While these doomsayers are predicting that 'the end is nigh', there are others who take a more uplifting and spiritual avenue towards the crises facing the human race as it approaches the Millennium.

Chapter Eight

Esoteric Prophecies

Rudolf Steiner on Prophecy

Rudolf Steiner (1861-1925) was an early Theosophist who created a profound and broad body of work encompassing spiritualism, healing, architecture, organic agriculture, education and many other fields, known as Anthroposophy. It has become a worldwide movement.

Steiner believed that prophecy is one of the highest forms of cognition and an essential part of humanity's spiritual development. In his book *Occult Science*, Steiner formulated spiritual laws which he compared to the laws that govern chemistry or physics, and utilized these principles to organize the psyche. Like Edgar Cayce he believed in the existence of the 'Akashic Record', containing the past of all humanity in its many forms and dimensions, and which can be tapped into through meditation and spiritual exercises.

Steiner felt that human development proceeded according to certain spiritual/evolutionary laws and that, once one's higher perception was able to comprehend them, the further developments of humanity could be prophesied. Indeed, he stated that this was an essential aspect of transcendent thought. As a 'scientist of the spirit', it is possible to foresee future great world events and human destinies without interfering with the choices involved in living in the future.

Steiner drew a distinction between predicting events through physical science and through spiritual perception. The physical sciences rely solely upon the intellect, composed of judgments, deductions, combinations and conclusions, while prophetic spiritual cognition proceeds from a higher seeing or perceiving.[1] This supersensibility allows the seer to gain access to higher worlds and preordain the directions of growth in human consciousness.

According to Steiner's timetable, we are currently in the middle of the fourth principal stage of human development, which is the condition of 'objective consciousness'. Before attaining our present state, humanity repeated successive cycles governed by the intelligences of the planets Saturn, the Sun and the Moon. We have just completed the transition from a consciousness which consisted of images, tones and colours within the soul, to one which is projected on to outside objects.

Humanity is already developing a disposition for higher states of consciousness, which will be used on the next planes, following the transformation of our present earthly existence. In the future the clairvoyant faculty will appear in a physical way, as a primary characteristic of consciousness, rather than as the dreamlike images typical of Moon-consciousness. When the Earth transforms itself into the next Jupiter stage, we will enter into concourse with beings hidden from our present sensory perception and who are the subjects of the 'mystery sciences'. At that stage there is no birth or death, only a unity of being with the cosmos.

Before the condition of Earth transforms into the life of Jupiter, there are three smaller cycles to be passed through, which will perfect consciousness. These will expose us to the Spirits of Personality (Primal Beginnings), the Sons of Fire (Archangels) and the Sons of Twilight (Angels). Similarly we will experience contact with the Seraphim, Cherubim and the Thrones, the true creators of humanity, who will reveal themselves to us.

As we are about to enter the Sixth Post-Atlantean epoch, the outer marks of race will diminish in importance, and individuality will be more characteristic. The root religions will be replaced by a Spiritual Science that will be practised over the entire Earth, without distinction of race or blood. We will lay aside the attributes of our 'group soul' and strive to contact spiritual guidance individually.

The Trans-Himalayan Wisdom

Madame H. P. Blavatsky identified the spiritual masters Koot Hoomi, Djwhal Khul and the Master Morya as the transmitting sources of her books *Isis Unveiled* and *The Secret Doctrine*, which formed the foundation of the Theosophical Society in the western esoteric tradition. Others who channelled from the same sources were Mabel Collins (*Light on the Path*) and Florence de la Rue. Both these women claimed their channel to be the senior disciple Hilarion, resident at the time in Egypt and Crete, and purported to be the transmitting source of the book of *Revelation* to John the Divine.[2] Countess Helena Roerich also received transmissions from the Master Morya, and her fifteen books written between 1924 and 1937 became the foundation of the Agni Yoga Society.

The modest, retiring and introvert Englishwoman Alice A. Bailey had her first contact with 'The Tibetan', Djwhal Khul, head of a lamasery in Shigatse, Tibet, in November 1919. The telepathic connection which she at first rejected outright became the centre of her life until her death in December 1949. In the intervening thirty years she wrote almost ten thousand pages in nineteen books on a range of esoteric subjects such as healing, astrology, psychology and the science of the Seven Rays, all dictated by The Tibetan.

In the beginning, her clairaudient communication with The Tibetan was laboured and slow, but through concentration and practice, she developed a crystal-clear transmission and could enter into telepathic communication instantly. She claimed that her books and the concepts contained therein were the work of The Tibetan, and not her own.

The nature and circumstances of Alice Bailey's transmissions of the teachings of The Tibetan followed a long-time connection with her own personally channelled teacher, the Master Koot Hoomi, the 'Master Who is very close to Christ', which had been established when she was a young girl, in November 1895. At that time she had revered Joan of Arc, and there are considerable similarities and parallels between the two young women. Djwhal Khul considered that she was continuing the tradition of the Trans-Himalayan Wisdom, following the precedent of Madame Blavatsky.

All of these women were channels for the transmission of the Secret Doctrine passed on for millennia within the Himalayas, fragments of which were periodically communicated to the outside world. This wisdom was also called the 'Perennial Philosophy' by Leibnitz and was the title of a book by Aldous Huxley. The basic idea of this philosophy is that behind the things, lives and ideas of the world is a divine, transcendent ground of reality, the nature of which cannot be perceived directly except by those who have fulfilled certain conditions — primarily being loving and pure of heart, like Parsifal, the knight of the Holy Grail.

The primal truth is available to everyone but is only recognized by the few. Once the realization has occurred it can be seen clearly, not only in an individual being, but also by reflection in others. This eternal truth lies at the core of all the major world religions, revelations and philosophies. It is always the same, although couched in different languages and expressed through different cultures. In certain unique circumstances this divine quality shines through and illuminates consciousness.

Aldous Huxley believed that when philosophers or literary people write of such ideas, it is usually, if not exclusively, at second hand.[3] But every age has certain men and women who fulfil the correct conditions and gain access to immediate knowledge and understanding of this reality. We may often think of it as an alternative reality, but it is more justifiably the real reality behind appearances. Those who have access to it are considered to be prophets, saints, sages, or enlightened ones — they are characterized as having a direct link with the gods or God.

The Seven Rays of Evolution

The informing idea behind the teachings of the Secret Doctrine and The Tibetan is that there have been seven waves of evolution in the universe, corresponding to seven interconnected energy fields, the *Seven Rays*, ranging from the dense to the finely spiritual. These seven fields correspond on an outer level with the seven major planets in our solar system, and internally with the seven chakras or centres of energy within our bodies. There are vibratory communications which link all these levels of being within us and between us. A life wave is contained within each of the planets and its energies, emanating from their planetary and spiritual intelligences. The proportion of the various seven waves and their degree of integration and interconnection determines the quality of our life.

According to the Hindus, a complete cycle of manifestation of the seven energies is a *Manvantara*. We are presently in the Fourth Manvantara of existence. Each Manvantara is composed of seven Yugas, and our present Yuga is the Kali Yuga, the Iron Age or the Yuga of Pain. The time periods embraced by this concept are truly astronomical as each Manvantara lasts for tens of millions of years.

Through Alice Bailey, The Tibetan has written extensively about exactly where we are in the scheme of history, when we left the previous stage, and when we will transform to the next stage. Although the scheme sounds quite complex, an individual in 1982 in the United States would be represented as Solar System II, Earth Chain II, Globe IV, Round IV, Root Race V, Subrace VI (American).[4]

The influence of Alice Bailey's books and the ideas they carry are in the tradition of the biblical prophets and are revered by many people today all over the world. They have inspired the creation of an esoteric science of the seven rays which is the foundation of many organizations such as the Arcane School, the Lucis Trust, the Seven Ray Institute, and the New Group of World Servers. Psychosynthesis is a school of psychotherapy developed by the Italian Roberto Assagioli and based on the dynamics of the seven rays.

The Tibetan's Prophecies

Among the many transmissions of The Tibetan are prophecies which cover events which have already happened, as well as developments which are projected to come to pass over the next million or more years. To say they are far-ranging is an understatement.

The prophecies are also very complete for the period from 1919-82, when The Tibetan stated that a new age would begin to manifest. The prophecies are particularly accurate regarding the discovery and early use of atomic energy, medical advances and the general development of humanity. Some of the prophecies are dated, but the majority are not. We will therefore confine ourselves to those prophecies which are relevant to the present transition of the Millennium.

With regard to the prophecies announcing the beginning of the Age of Aquarius, the dating of the transitory phase is not exact. As early as 1931, Djwhal Khul stated that humanity was now entering the sign Aquarius, and yet in many prophecies he focuses on the year 1999 as a transitional point between Pisces and Aquarius.

In 1945 The Tibetan gave out *The Great Invocation* which invoked the powers of light, love and divine purpose irrespective of all religions, and in 1946 Alice Bailey wrote: '. . . the day is dawning when all religions will be regarded as emanating from one great spiritual source.' The differences between the major world religions are minor and their foundations are similar, emerging as they do from the same spiritual source.

It is worthwhile quoting *The Great Invocation* here as it is considered to be important by many people in countless countries across the globe.

The Great Invocation

From the point of Light within the Mind of God
    Let light stream forth into the minds of men.
        Let Light descend on Earth.
From the point of Love within the Heart of God
    Let love stream forth into the hearts of men.
        May Christ return to Earth.
From the centre where the Will of God is known
    Let purpose guide the little wills of men —
        The purpose which the Masters know and serve.
From the centre which we call the race of men
    Let the Plan of Love and Light work out
        And may it seal the door where evil dwells.
Let Light and Love and Power restore the Plan on Earth. [5]

Michal Eastcott in her book *The Spiritual Hierarchy of the World* states that The Great Invocation is a forerunner of the kind of interdenominational invocation which will be central to the spiritual methods of the New World Religion which will eventually emerge in Russia, unconnected with any regime or political ideology. [6]

The Esoteric Prophecies for Aquarius

Let the group serve as Aquarius indicates; let Mercury speed the group upon the upward Way and let Taurus bring illumination and the attainment of the vision; let the mark of the Saviour, as the group toils in Pisces, be seen above the aura of the group. [7]

According to Djwhal Khul, the precessional sign Aquarius will initiate the most amazing period in history. The following prophecies relate to the incoming energy of the Aquarian Age. This age will be based on group interplay, group idealism and consciousness, whereas the Piscean Age was focused upon personal consciousness and unfoldment.

Astral energies emanating from Aquarius will stimulate the astral body of humanity to the new coherency of a brotherhood which will ignore racial and national differences. Once started, this process will unify life into a perfect brotherhood over a period of a thousand years. At present the Aquarian energy is having a negative effect upon the rank and file of humanity while it is activating positively on the pioneers of spiritual evolution. The platform upon which the materialists stand will be shattered and will disintegrate, and new abilities and horizons will emerge to lead humanity. As The Tibetan states:

> The remainder of this century . . . must be dedicated to rebuilding the shrine of man's living, to reconstructing the form of humanity's life, to reconstituting the new civilization upon the foundations of the old, recognizing the structure of world thought, world politics, plus the redistribution of the world's resources in conformity to divine purpose. Then and only then will it be possible to carry the revelation further. [8]

The planetary Logos is well aware that for the first time the three major planetary centres, Shamballa, Hierarchy and Humanity, are in direct and unimpeded relationship, adjusted specifically to this stage of planetary history. This process will lead to the Earth eventually becoming a 'sacred' planet. The unfolding process will have a potent subjective and deeply spiritual effect upon every kingdom in nature and in the realm of super-nature.[9]

The focus in the New Age will be on healing, according to the seven statements governing the student's magical statements or techniques.

According to The Tibetan, Russia's role in the transition is as yet embryonic, as her real function lies far ahead, and her centre inclines more towards the East than the West. The noisy, cruel child will turn into a controlled humanitarian in adult life, and potent influences in the Russian horoscope indicate this.

Initiating Aquarius

The following prophecies relate to the last decade of the twentieth century and the first thirty years of the twenty-first century, the true transition phase into the Age of Aquarius.

1975-2000

1975-   The Tibetan states that during the last quarter of this century the Trans-
2000   Himalayan Lodge will inaugurate activity through agents he calls 'psycho-scientific egos'. Indeed, following the death of Alice Bailey, her husband Foster Bailey believed that she was '. . . planning her next incarnation, which will be soon.'[10] During the last years of the 1990s, the great Chinese sage Confucius will incarnate to superintend the work, and the primary focus of transcendent activity will be through developments in Russia.

The main development of the society will happen through the creation of various seed groups of disciples of the New Age which will work to externalize the work of the hierarchy.

1945-2245

1945-   The culmination of the final stage of the returning Christ's three-
2245   hundred-year mission began in 1945 and will extend into the next Millennium, requiring a reciprocal attention to and recitation of the Great Invocation. He will not demonstrate the perfected life of a Son of God in this age, but rather will appear as the Head of the Spiritual Hierarchy, meeting the need of nations for truth, right human relations and loving understanding. He will testify to the *fact* of the resurrection and the immortality of the soul — the emphasis shifting from *death* to *life*.

1990-2050

1990-   During the last decade of the twentieth century the teaching about
2050   Shamballa will be revealed. The Atlantic Charter and the Four Freedoms to express the will of the Hierarchy will be made manifest by the Disciples across the Earth.

New scientific theories will be developed by two children, one from the US and one from India, which will harness the higher reaches of the light spectrum and allow motion to result from the power of the human eye. A tangible rapport with the spirit world will be possible for the first time in history.

1999

During the transitional time between the Piscean and Aquarian Ages *1999* the astrological sign Libra will steadily come into a position of power. Towards the year 1999 there will be a consolidation of the forces of evil and materialism on Earth, which will cause stress for those carrying through the Plan. Individual selfishness will be superseded by group selfishness, so that the small forces of good will have to work all the harder.

2000-2025

After the collapse of decadent human institutions in the latter part of *1999-* the 1990s, the period up to the beginning of the next century will be *2000* dedicated to rebuilding the form of the life of humanity, reorganizing thought structures, redistributing resources and reforming political institutions. This will ultimately lead to the creation of a World Federation of Nations in about 2025. (This sounds very much like the next stage beyond the United Nations and the European Community.) Early in the next century an initiate will appear to carry on the teaching of the Hierarchy.[11]

2000-2100

The Living Christ will resurrect and lead humanity towards the Mount *2000-* of Ascension and the Pentecost will become truth. The first stage of *2100* the Aquarian Age will be influenced by and resonate with the energy of Saturn, governed by the Third Ray. This is the planet of testing, opportunity, and expression and its activity is definitive.

The message of the seven rays is reaching humanity during these exciting transitional years, and the work of the Hierarchy is proceeding according to the plan. This is the esoteric message of the coming of the Millennium.

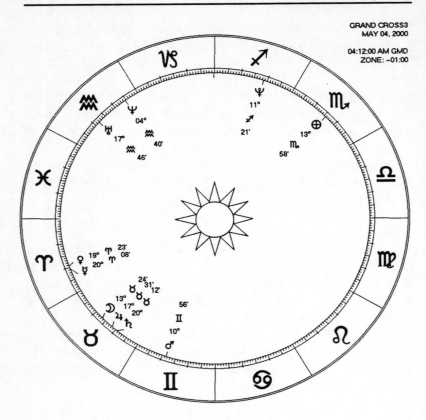

Figure 10. The Planetary Alignment of AD 2000
When shown as a heliocentric (sun-centred) diagram, in May 2000, the Earth and Pluto will be the only planets on their side of the Sun, with Uranus and Neptune midway between them. The stress on the Sun and its resultant activation of sunspots could create natural catastrophes at that time. (Computer horoscope © Matrix Software, Big Rapids, MI.)

Chapter Nine

Planetary Alignments, Earthquakes and Catastrophes

The 'Worst-Case Scenario'

A television documentary screened in Japan in 1980 and watched by many million Japanese presented the news that two eminent authorities had independently arrived at the conclusion that human life would be wiped off the face of the Earth in 1999.

The catalyst of these revelations was the integration of the prophecies of Nostradamus with the projections of the world's astronomers and astrologers about the famous Grand Cross which will occur in the solar system on 18 August 1999.

Professor Hideo Itokawa, who pioneered Japan's rocket technology, discovered through his computer calculations that on that date the Sun and the planets would take up the shape of a cross, a phenomenon which would coincide with the destruction of human society on Earth. Confirming the evidence garnered by his team of futurologist researchers, he forecast widespread environmental devastation caused by conflicts over energy and food resources. In his book *Case D*, the worst-case scenario for the world, he asserted that while he was unaware of Nostradamus' prophecies, he was a keen amateur astrologer and had written scholarly works about the phenomenon of the very rare Grand Cross.

The Uranus-Neptune Conjunction of 1993

It is the business of astrologers to make predictions, and many have predicted what will happen in the years approaching the Millennium, in addition to describing the significance of the major planetary alignment of 1999. The first major astrological event which will introduce this potent period will be the Uranus-Neptune conjunction of 1993. It is a rare meeting of these two powerful planets, happening only every 171 years, and its impact is being felt in the world even now.

The San Francisco astrologer Jim Lewis, who developed the revolutionary technique called AstroCartoGraphy, which maps planetary positions across the world, suggests that the Total Eclipse of 11 July 1991 anticipates the exact conjunction of the outer planets Uranus and Neptune, which will occur three times in 1993[1]. The position of the eclipse was at 19 degrees of Cancer, exactly opposite the degrees in Capricorn activated several times by the Uranus-Neptune conjunction. He sees the eclipse as an opening manifestation of the conjunction, which is one of the three rarest between the outer planets. It is generally accepted that humanity will feel the influences of this conjunction for about two or three years leading up to its exactitude in 1993. The exact dates for the conjunction are 2 February 1993, 20 August 1993 and 24 October 1993. In recent decades it is second only in importance to the Uranus-Pluto conjunction in Virgo in 1965, which produced sweeping changes in consciousness.

Uranus and Neptune were the first 'outer' planets to be discovered — Uranus in 1781, between the time of the American and French Revolutions, and Neptune in 1846, around the time when Karl Marx formulated the *Communist Manifesto*. As the planets from the Sun through Saturn are considered 'personal' planets, so the outer planets, which govern generational changes and a longer time perspective, have come to be seen as 'collective' influences.

Uranus is the planet associated with intuitive mental processes, breakdown and rapid change, particularly for groups and nations, and its transformation is usually accompanied by extremes of behaviour, unpredictable actions and even violence. Uranus corresponds to electricity because they were discovered at about the same time, and to technology in general, particularly such contemporary applications as computers and biological engineering, which are both extremely relevant issues in our own present day and for the future. Uranus also signifies the forces of democracy, free thinking and racial equality. Positive Uranian qualities are transformative, perceptive, regenerative and individualistic, while its negative qualities are disruptive, unpredictable, rash, violent, disordered and conflicting.

Neptune represents very different qualities, being associated with feeling and psychic processes, fantasy and spiritual idealism, Eastern philosophies, socialism, and new beliefs or understanding. Neptune governs alcohol and drugs and their use and abuse, whether pharmaceutical, recreational or harmful, as well as gases, pollution and disease. Negative Neptunian qualities are dissolution, lying and misinformation, disorganization, distorted beliefs, and corrupt spirituality.

The potential manifestations of the Uranus-Neptune conjunction are varied and complex, ranging from inspired experiences for humanity to confusion, chaos and the disintegration of systems. They could range from revolutionary scientific or technical discoveries, to contact with aliens, to the breakdown of civilization. The polarities embodied by Uranus-Neptune are thinking/feeling, West/East, Democratic/Socialist, Science/Religion and Analytical Psychology/Transpersonal Psychotherapy.

E. Alan Meece calls the Uranus-Neptune conjunction the 'cycle of cultural change' and believes it will have a profound effect upon all humanity in many ways, as do most astrologers.[2]

A primary field of influence for the conjunction is in international affairs, where a new order will emerge because the conditions which previously defined the conflicts of ideologies and religions between countries and continents will have been dissolved. We have already seen the disintegration of Communism as a world political order, leading to the voluntary dismantling of the Iron Curtain. This was symbolized by the final tearing down of the Berlin Wall erected after the Second World War, and the dissolution of the Soviet Union into the Commonwealth of Independent States. The underlying mechanism of the conjunction is the need for integration between the contrasting, if not opposed, Uranian democratic and Neptunian socialist ideologies. Mark Lerner suggests that the US is the planet's Uranian, Left Brain, Intellectual quality and that Russia is the planet's Neptunian, Right Brain, Psychic quality, and that the conjunction will lead to a unification, blending and integration of the two halves of the planetary brain. Therefore, 1993 could be an 'extraordinary opportunity for planetary, group and personal enlightenment'.[3]

Whereas outer planet aspects involving Pluto tend to manifest as wars and violent changes, Uranus-Neptune changes have been subtle and powerful, affecting the consciousness of entire nations and cultures rather than overtly outer events. The form of religious and racial attitudes and national identities is evolving and changing before our eyes, which in the long run can only be good. Previously fixed customs, as well as regional and national differences, become exaggerated and are on their way to resolution and integration. Religions are polarizing — either dissolving or becoming rigidly fundamentalist. Most national forms of government are drifting toward socialist (Neptune) democracies (Uranus), and those which are not are increasingly becoming international outcasts. Even the United States is being forced to revise their corrupt social charter towards equality. A new world order is emerging, and we have already seen the first signs.

Because of the revolutionary qualities of Uranus, modified by the diffused Neptune quality, the changes are likely to constitute fundamental alterations in consciousness about sexual, marital, racial, local, national and cultural identities, and we can see the evidence of this within what was the Soviet Union. The political might of Communism and the Communist Party held together the hundreds of small, ethnic cultures of the vast Soviet Union which would otherwise have been fighting each other as they had for hundreds of years before this century, and might into the next century. All the members of the new Commonwealth of Independent States are seeking to redefine their identity and to restore the deeply felt cultural, racial, religious and historical values which were forcibly suppressed for eighty years or more. In some cases this is an integrating influence, while in others, such as Armenia and Azerbaijan, it is the opposite, and old wounds are opened up.

It is for these reasons that the Uranus-Neptune conjunction is connected both with the dissolution of empires and kingdoms as well as the restoration of the same. As the USSR has broken down, so the possibility of a Russian royal family has returned. The Romanovs are returning to be embraced or buried in their native Russia. Similarly, after decades of exile, King Sianouk of Cambodia has returned, and the ruling families of many of the newly independent states in Asia and Europe are also lobbying for recognition and reinstatement. While this is not a serious possibility, it must be considered.

A historical manifestation of the Uranus-Neptune conjunction which parallels the present time was the creation by Charlemagne of the 'Holy Roman Empire' in AD 794. We might therefore expect to see a return to old orders and the recreation of supposedly defunct international organizations.

Another manifestation of the conjunction in this respect is the increased power of the United Nations and the European Community, symbolic of international alliances which are transcending formerly isolated social, racial, cultural and economic traditions. In the case of the UN, the paradox is that as it finally steps into the role of international forum for which it was intended, it is also flirting with bankruptcy. Both the UN and the EEC are becoming powerful forces to create a new order in the world. In the Security Council changes will be necessary to include Japan and the reunited Germany, as well as giving some consideration to how the new Commonwealth will be represented.

The conjunction of Uranus and Neptune in the sign Capricorn is in a square aspect relationship with Libra, the ruling sign of China. As other nations and continents are moving towards integration, the old guard in China are resisting the process, as was witnessed in the violent suppression of the democratic movement at Tiannanmen Square. In the last years of this century the movement in China will become so strong that the old men will not be able to resist the total change that will occur in that country.

A critical area in which the conjunction has influenced the world is that of the economy. The conjunction activates Capricorn, the sign of perfected matter and the domain of finance and business structures, and the economic state of the world is extremely unbalanced, and liable to irrational up and down swings.

As Uranus and Neptune are both associated with technology and ecological issues — Uranus representing machines, fossil-fuel burning and atomic technologies, and Neptune corresponding to chemicals, gases and water — their conjunction indicates a tendency toward ecological disasters. The use of CFCs and ozone-depleting chemicals has already caused irreversible damage to the ozone layer of the Earth. Already there are ozone holes above Australia, South America, the Poles, northern Europe and Scandinavia and the US, which are creating a vastly higher rate of skin cancers, eye cataracts and other health problems, not least of which is a weakening of the individual's immune system. The conjunction shows this issue coming to a critical point which will threaten our very survival. On a secondary level, it could bring an increase in computer viruses, disabling computers all over the world.

Uranus-Neptune will cause an increase in volcanic activity, such as the disastrous eruptions in the Philippines in 1991, which caused world-wide ecological effects and drastic changes in temperatures. As Uranus is associated with the electro-magnetic Earth energies criss-crossing the surface of the planet, and Neptune, symbolized by the god Poseidon, is water and the seas, their conjunction will create havoc between the two great ecological systems on Earth. Their conjunction is likely to correspond to periods of great heat, followed by excess water, floods and the washing away of land, patterns exactly like those which have been increasing all over the world in the last twenty years as a result of the ozone layer depletion.

On a more positive note, the Uranus-Neptune conjunction and its next 171 year cycle will also be a time for new beginnings, and for discoveries which will integrate the Uranian nature-science and the Neptunian spiritual-science. Eastern religious principles have already penetrated Western science in the writings and ideas of many physicists, not least of whom are Albert Einstein, Werner Heisenberg and David Bohm, and biologists such as Rupert Sheldrake, and they are set to have an even deeper effect upon our view of the universe. Beliefs will change dramatically and new discoveries which overlap into the psychic-spiritual domain will revolutionize modern thought and its applications in scientific and computer worlds. Thought-energy and fusion will be seen to be similar concepts, and radically new forms of energy could be found which will make our wasteful ways obsolete.

A primary application of the Uranus-Neptune principle will be in the area of healing and medicine which will cooperate with, and integrate, new ideas about the energy body and the potency of non-invasive remedies. A new view of world health will emerge which will give rise to a profound spiritual medicine for the twenty-first century.

The Major Planetary Alignment of 1999

Since the early 1970s there has been a greater than usual incidence of major earthquakes and volcanic eruptions on the Earth, and their effects upon the entire ecology of our planet is being felt in worldwide climatic changes. Initially scientists looked for geological causes for this increase, but during the 1970s and 1980s they discovered that the

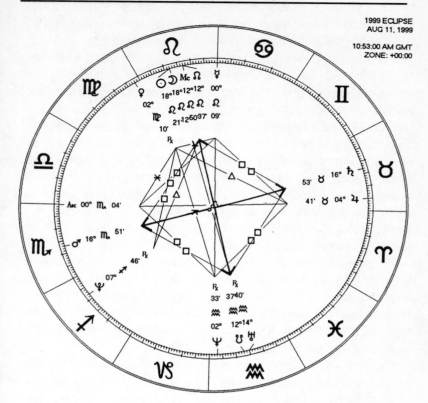

Figure 11. The 1999 Eclipse

In August 1999, there will be a Grand Cross of planets in the fixed signs related to the four beasts of the Apocalypse — Taurus the bull, Leo the lion, Scorpio the eagle, and Aquarius the man. The stress of this unique shape and its fixity could generate extreme unrest, violence and natural catastrophes such as earthquakes and tidal waves. (Computer horoscope © Matrix Software, Big Rapids, MI)

increase of earthquakes was related to sunspot cycles. The concentration of earthquakes seems to correspond to times when sunspots are most numerous, and also to times when the planets of the solar system align in specific geometric ways.

The Sumerians, Babylonians and Egyptians paid much attention to astrology, both to produce horoscopes and also to attempt to determine why major events happened in their world. The planets *were* gods and as such exerted power over the people's lives in many ways. They observed the planets, built temples to them, worshipped them and made them central to their histories and myths.

It has emerged in recent years that the effect the planets have on terrestrial events has been underestimated. In *The Jupiter Effect*, the scientists John Gribbin and Stephen Plagemann proved that the planets had an effect upon geological events on Earth. They predicted an increase in the number of earthquakes which would accompany a rare alignment of planets in 1982, and there was indeed unprecedented earthquake activity at that time. In this unusual alignment all of the planets, with the exception of the Earth (and the Moon, of course) were on one side of the Sun, close to where they will be in 1999. The intensification of activity observed in California and elsewhere at that time corresponded with an increase that had occurred in 1803, when there had been a similar alignment.

The planetary cause of such disturbances was originally investigated by Dr John Nelson of RCA Communications, who recognized that when any three of the nine planets are aligned in 90° or 180° geometric relationships, radio disturbances are greater, even when there are few sunspots. When more of the planets are involved in the alignment, the static is more pronounced.

The positions of the planets around the Millennium year 1999 could pose an even greater threat to the Earth. There will be an important eclipse, the last eclipse of the twentieth century, on 11 August 1999. This eclipse will activate a Grand Cross of planets in the fixed signs of the zodiac — Taurus, Leo, Scorpio and Aquarius — which correspond to the four beasts of the Apocalypse of the book of *Revelation*. Because of the exactitude of the cross and the inclusion of the destructive planets Mars, Saturn and Uranus, it could precipitate natural and human catastrophes.

Early in the Millennium year 2000, the Earth will be with Pluto on one side of the Sun (see Figure 10 on page 104), and a number of planets, including Mercury, Mars, Jupiter and Saturn, will align themselves in a straight line on the other side. NASA studies support the fact that solar activity also increases by more than 20 per cent when Jupiter and Saturn are involved in such alignments, because they are the two largest planetary bodies after the Sun. This alignment could therefore easily result in increasingly violent and destructive earthquakes and tidal waves, or even a shift of the world's axis.

Uranus is a critical factor in earthquake timings.[4] When Uranus is near the upper or lower transit of the meridian of the epicentre of earthquakes, they tend to be more powerful than otherwise. In the year 1999, Uranus is critically involved in the planetary alignment, and therefore could trigger off a disastrous series of earthquakes that could alter the balance of the Earth itself. The possibility of a shift of the poles was envisioned by the Biblical prophets and seen by Edgar Cayce — we must hope that their projections are wrong.

Psychic Predictions Approaching the Year 2000

Cayce and other psychics seem to agree on many of the changes in the world approaching the year 2000 (*see* Figure 9). Among those mentioned in *The Earthquake Generation* are the following:

- There will be a shift of the Polar Axis.
- A new climate will be established.
- Ancient cities will be found in the wake of falling seas.
- There will be major disturbances on both coasts of the US.
- Major sections of the US will fall into the sea — a final coast-line will be established in Nebraska.
- There will be major subsidence from Florida to Texas.
- There will be major earthquakes in Turkey and Yugoslavia.
- The Gulf Stream will undergo a complex shift.
- Some parts of the British Isles will submerge, while others will rise. London will be a coastal town.
- Land will rise in the North Sea, as Norway, Sweden, Denmark and Finland will have repeated coastal inundations.
- Most of Hawaii and Japan will break away.

While these projections are quite extreme, they correspond very closely with the entire range of prophecies for the Millennium we have seen expressed by prophets dating back to Biblical times. If they are true, the scientists will be forced to reacquaint themselves with the theories of cyclical cataclysms which were popular before Darwin.

Chapter Ten

The New Age

We are approaching the Age of Aquarius, a time of fundamental change which will affect all humanity. The precessional transition has always given rise to millennial expectations but, unfortunately, there is confusion about exactly when the changes from sign to sign occur. The reason for this is that the zodiac constellations are not exact 30 degree divisions of the ecliptic in the sky, but are haphazard star groups of various sizes. Constellations such as Scorpio occupy almost three times more than their expected twelfth of the zodiac belt. The fact that there may only have been ten astrological signs in ancient times has been postulated because of the extensive size of the constellations Scorpio and Virgo. Libra the Balance may have been created to mediate between the two when the zodiac was increased.

Dates for the Beginning of the Age of Aquarius

In *The Book of World Horoscopes*[1] Nicholas Campion mentions at least seventy dates for the beginning of the Age of Aquarius covering a range of 1500 years. He forewarns his readers by stating that there has been much confusion over this issue, and quotes the noted astrologer Charles Carter's statement that more rubbish has been written about this subject than any other branch of astrology, which is probably, in itself, an exaggeration.

As an illustration, Campion mentions an interesting synchronicity that occurred in 1962 involving a nineteenth-century French hoaxer and the renowned American clairvoyant Jeanne Dixon. In the 1890s Gabriel Jogand, primarily to agitate superstitious Catholics, deliberately devised and publicized a myth that the Antichrist was going to be born in 1962. On the projected day seventy years later, Jeanne Dixon had a vision that somewhere in the Middle East a baby had been born who would become a world teacher and lead humanity away from Christianity — an accurate definition of the Antichrist. Contemporary commentators saw this as the birth of a world teacher, and also as a symbol of the beginning of the Age of Aquarius.

Campion constructed the horoscope computed from Dixon's estimated time and transposed it to Jerusalem,[2] and discovered that there had been a Solar Eclipse on the previous day, when all the seven traditional planets were in the sign Aquarius. This is an interesting possibility for the entrance of the Age of Aquarius, but was not accompanied by any significant world events which would justify such a selection. This is also true of the majority of the dates previously set for this momentous entrance — that although enticing, they have not been persuasively connected with any major world events which would justify their claims. However, it could be reasoned that the entrance into the Age of Aquarius is an inner, rather than an outer transformation, which could be the case.

Many of the following proposed dates for the transition into the New Age of Aquarius are symbolic rather than astronomical or astrological, based as they are on intuitive datum points or perceived transitions.

Among the more obvious suggestions for the beginning of the Age of Aquarius are the following.

1898   According to Hindu chronology, the Kali Yuga (Age of Iron) began in the year 3102 BC. As the yuga has a duration of 5000 years, its end occurred in 1898.

1904   Aleister Crowley in *The Book of the Law*, dictated to him by a discarnate Egyptian entity, proposed April 1904 in Cairo, when the channelling occurred, as the beginning of the 'New Aeon' ruled by Horus, the solar god of ancient Egypt.

1905   Gerald Massey used the standard precessional period of 2160 years for each zodiac sign of 30° and assumed a starting point of 255 BC, which meant that the beginning of the Age of Aquarius was in 1905.[3] He used the correct precessional period, but his starting point seems only to be justified because it is significant for Massey, rather than for humanity as a whole.

1911   Madame Blavatsky predicted that the reality of a Universal Church would become possible towards the close of this century.[4] The Theosophical Society based their calculation for the dawning of the Age of Aquarius on the channelling of the Lord Maitreya by Krishnamurti in 1911.

1921   The Jockey Club of Barcelona received tremendous backing for a prediction that the world would end at this time.[5]

1936   Edgar Cayce stated that during 1936 the terrestrial axis had begun to shift, an exorable process which would activate the transition between world ages. The change would accelerate rapidly, with catastrophic consequences. A well-known American geologist confirmed that this axis shift did indeed begin below the Earth's surface in 1936.[6]

1945   Alice Bailey determined that the transition to the Age of Aquarius occurred in the 1930s as described in *The Externalisation of the Hierarchy*.[7] In 1945 the Master Djwhal Khul gave out The Great Invocation which invoked the powers of Light, Love and Divine Purpose irrespective of all religions, and in 1946 Alice Bailey wrote '. . . the day is dawning when all religions will be regarded as emanating from one great spiritual source.' (See pp. 99–100)

1962   Peruvian spriritual messenger Willaru Huayta of the Quechua Nation, a part of the ancient Inca confederation believes that the Age of Aquarius began in February 1962.[8]

1975   Rudhyar designated 1975 as the time when the Avatar of the New Age would appear. He allowed the possibility that it might not be the Second Coming of Christ anticipated by many, but that the Christ energy could be carried by a series of individuals who would be agents for this message.[9]

1975   A. Woldben in *After Nostradamus*[10] suggested a range of dates including 1975, 2000, 2023 and 2160. He stated that the transition of world ages is never exact and can take hundreds of years because they constitute a modification in collective consciousness.

1987   In August José Argüelles organized the 'Harmonic Convergence' which was a foretaste of the imminent New Age.

1997   Carl Jung was inspired by the work of Nostradamus and supported his contention that the New Age would happen between 1997 and 2000.

2000   There are many prophecies which agree that the Millennium year is 2000, among them those of Nostradamus, Edgar Cayce, St. Malachy, Garabandal, Fatima and other Christian prophets.[11] Margaret Hone in *The Modern Textbook of Astrology* gives the year 2000 as a 'symbolic date' for the New Age.[12] The seer Catherine Emmerich believed that Lucifer would be unchained 50 or 60 years before the year 2000.[13] The theory of *The Divine Plot*, by this author, is an astrological model of the historical process expressing multiple cyclic world ages, and it projects a transition to a new world age in the year 2000.[14]

2001   G. Barbarin stated that according to the principle of the Great Week and the six days of a thousand years of the adamic Era, there will follow a day of rest, the Millennium, which from the year 2001 will bring a thousand years of peace.[15] While his prophecy echoes the Seventh Day Adventists, it is also similar to the Hebrew Jubilee Year and Nostradamus' Seventh Millennium.

2010   Peter Lemesurier in *The Gospel of the Stars* suggests this as an 'official deadline'[16] and entrance into the Age of Aquarius. He quotes the French Institut Géographique National for support of his claim.

2012   Terence and Dennis McKenna in *The Invisible Landscape*[17] advance an idea derived from studies of primitive shamanism and psychoactive drugs that our universe is created by the holographic interaction between two hyper-universes, and that the Universe is cyclic and recurrent. Based on extensive computer modelling, they think that humanity will experience a 'Resurrection into the Light' during six days in AD 2012 when, in the last 135 minutes, eighteen barriers, comparable to the appearance of life, the invention of language or the achievement of immortality will be experienced, thirteen of them in the last millisecond.

2012   José Argüelles discovered a system of cycles based on the ancient Mayan calendar (Figure 12), and determined that the

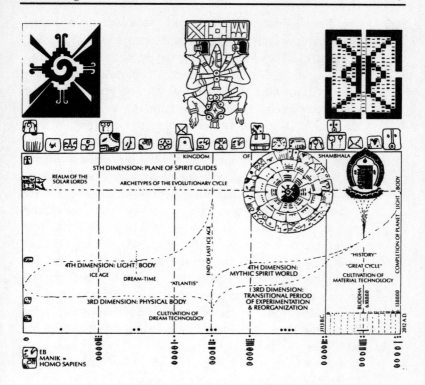

Figure 12. The 26,000-Tun Cycle
We are experiencing the last decades of a 26,000-year cycle of *Homo sapiens*, when the Light Body of the Earth will be complete. The date of completion, AD 2012, is on the right of this diagram. (Argüelles, *The Mayan Factor*)

year AD 2012 would be the end of the 396-year Baktun of the Transformation of Matter, the collapse of global civilization and the Earth purification and regeneration of the planet, with a following era of information and crystal-solar technology and galactic synchronization.[18]

2020   Adrian Duncan proposed the 'Aquarian Mutation' chart, a horoscope for the Aquarian transition, being the time when Jupiter and Saturn are conjunct in Aquarius for the first time since AD 1404. (21 December 2020, 18.18 GMT, as published in *Doing Time on Planet Earth*.[19])

2025   The Tibetan Djwhal Khul, speaking through Alice Bailey,
        stated that the Fourth Ray comes into manifestation in 2025,
        bringing qualities for preparing for the discrimination and
        balance required for the intellectual and emotional refine-
        ment of humanity. Humanity will then be able to function
        more completely on the intuitional plane.

2059   Rudhyar in *The Lunation Cycle*. There is a disagreement over
        this and the following date in Rudhyar's work.

2060   Dane Rudhyar determined that the last precessional Age of
        Pisces began in 100 BC, and since a world age is 2160 years,
        the official Age of Aquarius begins in this year.[20] He
        considered that the last 10 per cent of each age is its 'Seed
        Period' during which its influence will begin to be felt and
        experienced. He mentions that in 1844 a young Persian
        prophet announced the end of the Islamic era and the
        beginning of the New Age, the avatar of which would
        announce himself some nineteen years later. One of his
        original followers proclaimed himself *Baha'u'llah* ('Glory of
        God'), the Expected One. And, in 1846 the planet Neptune
        was also discovered.

        Rudhyar believed that the new cycle had already started
        to release its spiritual-archetypal energies, which are now
        making their way downward into manifestation, producing
        a radical upheaval of public institutions focusing around the
        time of the massing of planets in the sign Capricorn, the ruler
        of large-scale political organizations. This would constitute
        a 'rite of passage' for all humanity and, in the destruction of
        existing and faulty ways of perceiving and organizing the
        world, humanity would discover a new way of life.

2160   Gordon Strachan in *Christ and the Cosmos* follows the
        standard precessional age of 2160 years using the birth of
        Christ as his datum point.[21]

2874   Based on his mathematical analysis of the Great Pyramid
        passages, Morton Edgar set this date as the completion of
        Christ's 'Day of Restitution' when the world will have gained
        all it has lost throughout history.

2915   Edgar stated that in this year, forty years after the preceding
        date, the Redeemed Race will experience to the full the

glorious liberty of the children of God, with complete dominion over the Earth.

The dates and attributions stretch all the way ahead to Robert Hand's use of precessional movement combined with the actual size of the constellation Pisces in the sky, to arrive at the date of AD 2813, and beyond to the year 3550.

It is clear from the preceding that the date of the entrance into the Age of Aquarius is anything but definite and it would seem that almost everyone has his or her version of the exact point. It is certain that the transition is in the process of taking place and it will have a great impact upon all humanity.

The Christian Symbolism of the Piscean Age

We are now experiencing the end of the Age of Pisces, which has lasted from the birth of Jesus Christ to the present, as we approach the Millennium year 2000. Jesus was the incarnation and symbol of the entire age. Astrologically, as a Piscean avatar, he contained the opposite sign Virgo, as exemplified by his virgin birth from his mother Mary.

The coming of the Christ had been prophesied for centuries before his birth as the cross-over point between the preceding Arian Age and the Piscean Age. God chose to incarnate and create as his vehicle his own son, whereas God had previously only been accessible through arcane priesthoods or anointed god-kings. For the first time the holy presence existed incarnate, and humanity took this message to its heart.

During the two thousand years which have elapsed since the beginning of the Piscean Age, the message of Jesus Christ has been followed and also abused. The Church became so enamoured of its own power that it developed in overtly un-Christian directions. Piety among Christians has decreased in favour of material wealth, dishonesty and lust; and outward appearances have virtually submerged the essential values central to the Christian message.

The Church founded by St Peter became dominant through the message of his spiritual Master, Jesus Christ. Both men would have been horrified at the acts perpetrated in their names over the centuries, as indeed they would have been pleased by the great good also done through and on behalf of the church. But now, as the Age of Pisces ends, humanity awaits a New Age.

The New Aquarian Age

One dominant message of the New Age is that an avatar, probably the Christ, catalyst of the outgoing Piscean Age and redeemer of its humanity, will be reborn, either in symbolic form or as an actual reincarnation, a Second Coming. Several prophets have predicted just such a coming, one of the most recent being Benjamin Creme in London, who anticipated the arrival of Jesus Christ from within the Pakistani population of East London in the 1980s.

Many accept that the 'seed beings' who will initiate the New Age are already here. When the rhythms of the cosmic ages group together, concentrating as they do at the ends and beginnings of World Ages, certain individuals are born to husband and nurture these energies. They are focal points and channels through whom the messages of the new humanity are expressed and made manifest.

It is clear that the teachers from the Piscean Age have lost their influence. The influence of Christianity is at an all-time low. Those raised as Christians are being drawn to a spectrum of alternative religious beliefs, from shamanism or Native American ritual, to Eastern religions. The Church is seen as being corrupt. Some other world religions have been dominated by reactionary and revolutionary political ideologies. The gurus of the 1960s and 1970s have disappointed, and faded out of the limelight. Their withdrawal has often been dramatic, as in the disappointment over the claimed avatar status of Krishnamurti, or the lines of Rolls Royces and the frenzy of misunderstanding in the case of Bhagwan Sri Rajneesh. In both cases they were wise men whose time came and then passed. The time for journeys to the East has passed also. Eastern wisdom is now around us and within us. It is an integral part of the new world order — spiritually, philosophically, artistically, economically and scientifically. A new level of integration is required, and it is already happening.

The decline and dissolution of Communism is symbolic of the limitations of political movements. Since the middle of the nineteenth century, political ideologies have taken the place of religion, and they are now collapsing in what people perceive as a torrent of greed, abuse, inequality, corruption and disdain for the truth. In America this has been symbolized by the assassination of John F. Kennedy, and the subsequent humiliation of Richard Nixon. There is little if any regard for the President of the United States, except as a figurehead for big business, and people wonder what will happen now that the Cold War has ended. The time is near for the influence of the people to be felt.

The rights of former minority groups are being examined closely, particularly because they are actually majorities. The Women's Movement of the 1970s has been followed by variations on a Men's Movement in the 1990s, both being an attempt to redefine the position, aspirations and psychological relationship of the sexes. History is being rewritten, taking into consideration those whose influence had previously been ignored or abused. Similarly, in a world perspective, racial and religious groups are moving towards a unity and dissolution of barriers. This may be threatening for many people, but it will lead to a greater world brotherhood and sisterhood. A new pattern of being is evolving before our eyes.

The decline in influence of spiritual teachers or gurus on a global scale has meant that the wisdom of the ages is increasingly seen to reside within the individual, within the family, within the smaller units of our societies. The new wisdom is above or beyond being either Eastern or Western, available or esoteric, Buddhist or Christian, astrological or psychological — it is heartfelt and individual. It is as though the collective heart chakra of humanity has been opened.

The population explosion has meant that as many people have lived in the twentieth century as have lived in all history, back to the time 50,000 years ago, when the conscious Cro-Magnon humans emerged for the first time. Humanity is increasing in numbers and time is accelerating towards the Millennium year. The accelerating pace of the modern world is so great that few can stand the density of living. Indeed, it is difficult not to feel the great explosion of people, information and energy as well as the pain and hunger this has caused, and will continue to cause.

Accompanying this population explosion has been a renewal and rediscovery of many primary religious movements and beliefs, customs, myths and folk wisdom, symbols and identifications, from all over the world and from all times. No one seems able to imagine what our future will look like, because we are looking to the past for our answers. There is a lack of vision as to what the world will be like or look like in twenty years' time.

The New Jerusalem

John Michell's *City of Revelation* describes a perennial philosophy which is based on the interpretation of the magical numerology of the Bible, allied with an understanding of megalithic astronomy, translated into the concept of a coming New Jerusalem. Using the key numbers 666 and 1080, which are prominent in the numerology of the book of *Revelation*, Glastonbury, Stonehenge and other great monuments, Michell proposes that the Temple of Jerusalem (Figure 13) is a metaphor for the Earth itself, and that the restoration of the Temple is no less than a rebirth of the Earth spirit and represents the return of the age of prophecy and the return of divine revelation.

Through a careful analysis of the structure and measurements of Glastonbury, Stonehenge and reconstructions of the Temple of Jerusalem, Michell describes the degeneration of the intelligence which created them and the current revival of those same spiritual energies. He feels that the present neglect of sacred history in favour of the secular is a denial of God and the gods. While aware of the cataclysmic projections made by many about what is to happen in our near future, he also allows that the true prophet may see the germs of a return to the New Jerusalem and the gods entering into the Age of Aquarius. Fluxes of cosmic radiation, which are typical of such changes in world ages, will accelerate the changes.

The desire for a new revelation is very seductive in our time. New Age pioneers believe that the rising influence of the gods, restored to their rightful place in the scheme of things, will catalyze the psychic changes required to alter the existing world order. Yet Michell recognizes the millennial signals symbolizing hopeful expectations.

Michell identifies the forces of science and industry as the factors primarily responsible for the current state of our world. He compares them with the image of Babylon, leading to the realization that the destruction of Babylon is a necessary antecedent to the creation of the New Jerusalem. He also identifies the need for the Millennium and its

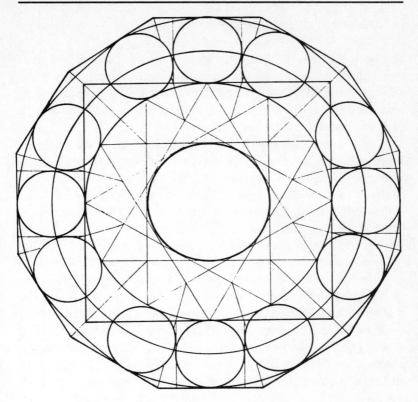

Figure 13. The New Jerusalem
The New Jerusalem as revealed by St John in *Revelation* 21 is created
from the geometry and cycles of terrestrial and lunar spheres. This
diagram by John Michell portrays the geometry underlying the New
Jerusalem and locates the twelve gates corresponding to the zodiac
signs and the length of the precessional Platonic month of 2160
years. (John Michell, *City of Revelation*)

signs as being an archetypal quality of humanity.

We are currently seeing the conflict between the powers of solar
radiation signified by the force of the number 666, and the spiritual
perception, humility and freedom inherent in the number 1080. The
fruits of this struggle are symbolized by their sum of 1746, which
symbolically is the grain of mustard seed from which grow the roots
and branches of the great cosmic tree, the symbol of cosmic unity.[22]

Native American Indian Prophecies

The Native American Indians had lived in North America, on what they called 'Turtle Island', for many thousands of years before the Vikings came in AD 1100 and Columbus in 1492. Many tribes wandered across the vast spaces, hunting and living in balance with each other and the abundant nature around them.

Integral to the teachings of these Native Americans is that all things are related, and all actions in the entire web of life influence all others — they lived their lives in accord with this sacred law. Modern science has only recently discovered and acknowledged this essential fact with Relativity and the Superstrings Theories, but all Native Americans learn about it in childhood.

The Native American sages have known for centuries, since before the appearance of the white man, that a sinister force would arrive in their land. Ancient prophecies foretold of a wandering away from the sacred path followed by the original Native Americans, symbolized by a series of fires. During the Fourth Fire, light-skinned people would come to Turtle Island wearing the face of brotherhood. They would usher in an exciting time and bring new inventions and knowledge, and they would integrate the smaller nations into four larger nations, and then the four into one powerful nation. The prophets warned;

> Beware if the light-skinned race comes wearing the face of death. You must be careful because the face of death and the face of brotherhood look very much alike.[23]

Other prophets said that they would bring suffering, and that the proof would be seen in rivers running with poison and fish becoming unfit to be eaten. These prophets have been right — as of 1990 there were over fourteen hundred dead lakes in Canada alone.

The Native American prophets correctly predicted the wars when their brothers and sisters would be killed by great armies, and their children turned away from the teachings of their elders. Their people would be forced to choose between the two roads available to them — the road to technology and the road to spirituality. The people would only be free again by choosing the road to spirituality and rediscovering the ways of the elders again, within themselves.

The Hopi prophets have foreseen the world wars, the invention of automobiles and aeroplanes, and even the atom bomb, and that the sons of white men would grow their hair long and live in communal societies.[24] They called these men and their kin, who would come to the elders to learn the healing arts, the 'Rainbow Warriors'. They are composed of every colour and race on the planet, as no pure blood remains anywhere. Part of their task is to show humanity that they are all the same, all members of the same tribe. The Hopis wish that all such Rainbow Warriors will become spiritual warriors and help heal the Earth and restore the balance of nature.

Upon being shown pictures of the crop circles recently discovered all over Europe and America, the Hopi elders recognized the patterns and symbols as communications from the Earth Mother herself, crying dirty tears (polluted waters) about her lost blood (oil removed from the ground), and saying that she is dying from suffocation (air pollution). She is trying to be heard in her pain, and we must listen.

Sun Bear and the Earth Changes

According to Sun Bear, a member of the Chippewa Nation at the White Earth Reservation in northern Minnesota, his people tell of journeys through the four worlds. Each world ends and is joined to the next world by a time of cleansing. The Migration Scrolls show that we are presently in the cleansing before the last of the worlds. 'The death of the forests, the poisoning of the waters, the shaking of the Earth . . ,' were all foreseen by the native prophets. Sun Bear therefore is teaching people to survive during the time of the Earth changes to come. Sun Bear prophesies that between now and the year 2000 there will be three years when there will be practically no food on the planet, and that we must prepare ourselves for this time.

Willaru Huayta and the Ancient Incan Prophecy

The Inca Indian prophecies (as transmitted by Willaru Huayta, a Peruvian descended of the Quechua Nation) reflect their ancient solar, cosmic, universal religion. The tradition remains alive, particularly in the Amazon jungle, the final retreat and sanctuary of the wisdom tradition of the Incan Empire.

The Incan prophecies say that over the last five hundred years the eagle of the North and the condor of the South have been flying separately, and when they fly together, as is beginning to happen now, people will begin to speak from the heart again. The Incan traditions embrace the ideals of Atlantis, the early culture on Earth which was destroyed by a great cataclysm thousands of years ago. The survivors of this enlightened world age created the nucleus of their civilization in South America, among other places. But their religion was corrupted by the arrival of the Spaniards, who were enemies of the Sun, and humanity has degenerated since then. Scientists cannot see the multidimensional world of the spirit which is at the core of the ancient ways, and materialism has become dominant. As long ago as 1750, the grand Inca Shora Atahuallpa warned the soldiers of the Sun that humanity will break its connection to the natural forces, will lose its way, and the people will become lost in darkness.[25] But changes are already in progress.

His visions have shown that humanity entered the Age of Aquarius in 1962, and that this fifth solar generation is in its early stages of development. Between 1962 and the Harmonic Convergence of 1987, certain people began to receive messages and have their inner powers activated so that they could complete their mission on Earth. He states that:

> Cataclysm is coming now in this time of transition, but there's no need to worry about it. The Earth will shake, the air will be filled with hurricanes and tornadoes, the ocean will have huge waves, and the Sun will have great heat. The year 2013 is the end of the Incan calendar.[26]

According to Huayta, the cataclysm will come in the year 2013, when a big magnetic asteroid, three times larger than Jupiter, will come close to Earth and its force will activate the cleansing of the Earth. When the cataclysm is over, the seed people will return and begin a new civilization. The fifth generation will disappear with the cataclysm, but we can be the seed of the sixth generation, if we can only contact and bring alive the light within us.

The End and Beginning of History

It is thought by some that we are experiencing the End of History — if history means the process by which humanity has developed, fought, diversified and differentiated itself on its way to the here and now. The distinctions characterizing the two major political systems for the last century — democracy and socialism/communism — are dissolving. Their fundamental polarity has diminished. Either integration or stalemate remains.

As the disintegrating USSR treads the path to democracy, so the United States Congress attempts to pass legislation which would socialize its health and economic systems. These reciprocal changes are urgently needed, but seem destined to polarize into deeper problems first. It is as though the elements within each society are now reflecting divisions which were formerly projected on to their enemies outside. The opponents on both sides of the Iron Curtain are realizing that they are one: seer and shadow. We must now get to work on the barriers within us which are preventing us from living the quality of life we should expect from our world.

In psychology the concept of the 'shadow' is primary. We all have a dark side, on to which we project all the unknowingness we feel, the difficult and awkward parts of ourselves, our futility, our powerlessness, and also our anger and murderous instincts. Everything we suppress is there, waiting for the floodgates to open so that it can push out and dominate our lives. In the early stages of the psychotherapeutic process our unconscious 'Pandora's Box' of suppressed memories is opened, and it feels as if we are dying. We feel this because our consciously controlled identity is shattered by these emerging feelings, and because we are forced to meet a part of ourselves which we do not want to see, or even acknowledge is there. It is easier to forget, to project our shadow qualities on to difficult partners, or parties which oppose our policies, the gurus who hold different beliefs, the teams which beat ours, and the lovers we cannot have. What we are witnessing in the world today is a collective manifestation of this phenomenon.

When our old enemies have become our friends; when the Cold War budgets and the justification for being armed are no longer there; when there is no reason to continue to pollute the environment; then the most difficult questions begin to be asked. When we begin to plumb the depths of our selves and discover how we can band together to stave off the destruction of our planet; when we can give away what we have to balance out the world resources with those who have not; then our true integration will begin.

Then we will have called on our inner teachers to find our inherent wisdom, to identify with the parts of us that know and care, rather than blaming the world for the situation we have created.

Then we will know that the New Age is Here.

Notes

Chapter One - The Nature of Prophecy

1. Mann, Thomas, *Joseph and His Brothers*, p. 18.
2. The work of Edgar Cayce is discussed in Chapter Seven, beginning on p. 79.
3. Michel de Nostradamus is discussed in Chapter Six, beginning on p. 51.
4. Collin, Rodney, *The Theory of Celestial Influence*, p. 350.
5. Ibid, p.352.

Chapter Two - Zodiacal Mysteries

1. Anonymous, *The Prophesies of Nostradamus*, pp. 19-20 and 27.

Chapter Three - The Millennium

1. From George Andrews, many years ago.
2. Cohn, Norman, *The Pursuit of the Millennium*, p. 21.
3. Scholem, Gershom, *Major Trends in Jewish Mysticism*, pp. 178-9.
4. Strachan, Gordon, *Christ and the Cosmos*, pp. 57-9.
5. Ibid, p. 72.

Chapter Four - Christianity and the Apocalypse

1. Puech, Henri-Charles, 'Gnosis and Time', *Man and Time*.
2. Mann, Sesti, Flanagan & Cowen, *The Phenomenon Book of Calendars*, p. 10.
3. Ibid, p. 48.
4. Cohn, Norman, p. 13.
5. *Revelation*, XXII:2 and XXII:6.
6. James, M R (trans.), *Apocryphal New Testament*, pp. 556-60.
7. Cohn, Norman, p. 25.
8. Ibid, pp. 8-11.
9. Dennis, Geoffrey, *The End of the World*, p. 105.
10. Ibid, p. 168.
11. Thomas, Keith, *Religion and the Decline of Magic*, p. 168.
12. Sesti, Mann, Flanagan & Cowen, p. 9.
13. Corbin, Henry, 'Cyclical Time in Mazdaism and Ismailism', *Man and Time*, p. 157.

Chapter Five - Prophecies of the Great Pyramid

1. Davidson and Aldersmith, *The Great Pyramid: Its Divine Message*, p. xvi.
2. West, John Anthony, *Serpent in the Sky*, pp. 22-3.
3. Davidson, pp. vi-vii.
4. Toth, Max, *Pyramid Prophecies*, pp. 220-22.
5. Edgar, Morton, *The Great Pyramid: Its Time Features*, p. 138.
6. Ibid, p. 235.

Chapter Six - Nostradamus and the *Centuries*

1. Cheetham, Erika, *The Prophecies of Nostradamus*, p. 13. This is the most valuable modern translation of the *Centuries*.
2. Ibid, p. 10.
3. Ibid, p. 38.
4. Ibid, pp. 48-9.
5. Anonymous, *The Prophesies of Nostradamus*, p. 45.
6. Ibid, p. 11.
7. Ibid, p. 78.
8. Ibid, pp. 6-16.
9. Ibid, footnote on p. 10.
10. Cheetham, Erika, p. 92.
11. Anonymous, p. 13.
12. Cheetham, Erika, p. 120.
13. Laver, James, *Nostradamus, or the Future Foretold*, p. 235.
14. Anonymous, *The Prophecies of Nostradamus*, p. 31.
15. Ibid, p. 31.
16. Laver, James, pp. 230-1.

Chapter Seven - Psychics, Seers and Mystics

1. Thomas, Keith, pp. 464-5.
2. Dennis, Geoffrey, pp. 112-15.
3. Carter, Mary Ellen, *Edgar Cayce On Prophecy*, p. 189.
4. Stearn, Jess, *Edgar Cayce: The Sleeping Prophet*, p. 82.
5. Ibid, p. 82.
6. ARE Index Code 3976-15, dated 19 January 1934.
7. Stearn, Jess, p. 45.
8. Ibid, p. 37-8.
9. Ibid, p. 46.
10. Carter, Mary Ellen, p. 166.
11. Fisher, Joe, with Peter Cummins, *Predictions*, p. 150.
12. Jung, C G, (trans. H G Baynes), *VII Sermones ad Mortuos*.
13. Between 15 December 1916 and 16 February 1917, in Hoeller, Stephen A, *The Gnostic Jung*.
14. Jung, C G, pp. 33-4.

Chapter Eight - Esoteric Prophecies

1. Steiner, Rudolf, *Cosmic Memory*, pp. 146-8.
2. Stephenson, James, *Prophecy on Trial*, p. 13.
3. Huxley, Aldous, *The Perennial Philosophy*, p. 2.
4. Stephenson, James, pp. 23-7.
5. Bailey, Alice A, *Telepathy*, p. ix.
6. Eastcott, Michal, *The Spiritual Hierarchy of the World*, p. 96.
7. Stephenson, James, p. 241.

8. Bailey, Mary, *A Learning Experience*, p. 27.
9. Stephenson, James, p. 242.
10. Bailey, Mary, p. 9.
11. Bailey, Alice, *A Treatise on the Seven Rays*, p. 4.

Chapter Nine - Planetary Alignments, Earthquakes and Catastrophes

1. Lewis, Jim, 'The Eclipse and the New World Order', *The Mountain Astrologer*, June 1991.
2. Meece, E. Alan, 'The Cycle of Cultural Change: The Uranus-Neptune Conjunction', *The Mountain Astrologer*, June 1991.
3. Lerner, Mark, 'The Uranus-Neptune Conjunctions Are Coming', *Welcome to Planet Earth*, Spring 1992, p. 4.
4. Goodman, Jeffrey, *The Earthquake Generation*, pp. 180-90.

Chapter Ten - The New Age

1. Campion, Nicholas, *The Book of World Horoscopes*, pp. 393-403.
2. Ibid, p. 394. Campion's published horoscope for the New Moon one day before the predicted birth is for 00:10 AM GMT, 5 February 1962, Jerusalem, Israel.
3. Rudhyar, Dane, *Astrological Timing: The Transition to the New Age*, p. 115.
4. Eastcott, Michal, p. 95.
5. Dennis, Geoffrey, p. 135.
6. Woldben, A, p. 201.
7. Bailey, Alice, *The Externalisation of the Hierarchy*, pp. 3-5.
8. McFadden, Steven, *Profiles in Wisdom*, p. 221.
9. Rudhyar, Dane, *Occult Preparations for a New Age*, p. 249.
10. Woldben, A, p. 34.
11. Ibid, p. 203.
12. Hone, Margaret, *The Modern Textbook of Astrology*, p. 293.
13. Ibid, p. 212.
14. Mann, A T, *The Divine Plot: Astrology and Reincarnation*.
15. Woldben, A, p. 212.
16. Lemesurier, Peter, *Gospel of the Stars*, p. 48.
17. McKenna, Terence and Dennis, *The Invisible Landscape*, p. 183-4.
18. Argüelles, José, *The Mayan Factor*, pp. 115-18.
19. Duncan, Adrian, *Doing Time on Planet Earth*, pp. 172-4.
20. Rudhyar, Dane, p. 132.
21. Strachan, Gordon, p. 111.
22. Michell, John, *City of Revelation*, p. 172.
23. McFadden, Steven, pp. 42-3.
24. Ibid, p. 134.
25. Ibid, pp. 217-21.
26. Ibid, p. 223.

Bibliography

Anonymous, *The Prophesies of Nostradamus*, Avenel Books, New York, 1975.
Argüelles, José, *The Mayan Factor*, Bear & Co., Santa Fe, 1987.
Asimov, Isaac, *A Choice of Catastrophes*, Arrow, London, 1981.
Bailey, Alice, *A Treatise on the Seven Rays*, Lucis, New York, 1936.
——, *Telepathy*, Lucis, New York, 1971.
Bailey, Mary, *A Learning Experience*, Lucis Trust, New York, 1983.
Blacker, Carmen and Loewe, Michael, eds., *Ancient Cosmologies*, Allen & Unwin, London, 1975.
Blavatsky, Helena Petrovna, *Isis Unveiled*, The Theosophy Company, Los Angeles, 1931.
——, *The Secret Doctrine*, The Theosophy Company, Los Angeles, 1947.
Bolin, Jean Shinoda, *The Goddesses in Everywoman*, Harper & Row, New York, 1984.
——, *The Gods in Everyman*, Harper & Row, New York, 1989.
Campbell, Joseph, ed., *Man and Time*, Bollingen, New York, 1957.
Campion, Nicholas, *The Book of World Horoscopes*, Thorsons, Wellingborough, 1988.
Capra, Fritjof, *The Turning Point*, Wildwood House, London, 1982.
Carter, Mary Ellen, *Edgar Cayce On Prophecy*, Warner Books, New York, 1968.
Cheetham, Erika, *The Prophecies of Nostradamus*, Spearman, London, 1973.
——, *The Final Prophecies of Nostradamus*, Futura, London, 1990.
Collin, Rodney, *The Theory of Celestial Influence*, Shamballa, Boulder, 1984.
Cohn, Norman, *The Pursuit of the Millennium*, Granada, London, 1970.
Corbin, Henry, 'Cyclical Time in Mazdaism and Ismailism', *Man and Time*, Eranos Yearbook 3, New York, 1957.
Crowley, Aleister, *Magical and Philosophical Commentaries on The Book of the Law*, 93 Publishing, Montreal, 1973.
Davidson, and Aldersmith, *The Great Pyramid: Its Divine Message*, Williams & Norgate, London, 1925.
Dennis, Geoffrey, *The End of the World*, Eyre & Spottiswoode, London, 1930.
Duncan, Adrian, *Doing Time on Planet Earth*, Element Books, Shaftesbury, 1990.
Eastcott, Michal, *The Spiritual Hierarchy of the World*, Sundial House, Tunbridge Wells, 1973.
Edgar, Morton, *The Great Pyramid: Its Time Features*, Bone & Hulley, Glasgow, 1924.
Ferguson, Marilyn, *The Aquarian Conspiracy*, RKP, London, 1982.

Ferrier, J. Todd, *The Message of Ezekiel*, Percy, Lund, Humphries, London, 1931.

Fisher, Joe with Peter Cummins, *Predictions*, Jonathan James, London, 1980.

Gattey, Charles Nelson, *Prophecy and Prediction in the 20th Century*, Aquarian Press, Wellingborough, 1989.

Goodman, Jeffrey, *The Earthquake Generation*, Turnstone, London, 1979.

Hall, Manley Palmer, *Secret Teachings of All Ages*, Philosophical Research Society, Los Angeles, 1968.

Hoeller, Stephan A., *The Gnostic Jung*, Quest, Wheaton, 1982.

Hogue, John, *Nostradamus & the Millennium*, Bloomsbury, London, 1987.

Hone, Margaret, *Modern Textbook of Astrology*, Fowler, London, 1971.

Huxley, Aldous, *The Perennial Philosophy*, Chatto & Windus, London, 1946.

James, M. R., (trans.), *The Apocryphal New Testament*, Oxford, 1924.

Jung, Carl G., (trans. H.G. Baynes), *VII Sermones ad Mortuos*, Stuart & Watkins, London, 1963.

King James Version, *Holy Bible*, Philadelphia, 1775.

Laver, James, *Nostradamus, or the Future Foretold*, Collins, London, 1942.

Lemesurier, Peter, *Gospel of the Stars*, Element Books, Tisbury, 1977.

_____, *The Great Pyramid Decoded*, Element Books, Tisbury, 1977.

Leti, Gentle, *Papyrus Anana*, collection of George Andrews.

Lewis, Jim, 'The Eclipse and the New World Order,' *The Mountain Astrologer Journal*, June/July 1991.

Mann, A. T., *Life*Time Astrology*, Allen & Unwin, London, 1984 and Element Books, Shaftesbury and Rockport, 1991.

_____, *The Divine Plot*, Allen & Unwin, London, 1986 and Element, Shaftesbury and Rockport, 1991.

_____,(Ed.), *The Future of Astrology*, Unwin Hyman, London, 1987.

Mann, Sesti, Flanagan and Cowen, *The Phenomenon Book of Calendars 1979-1980*, Anchor/Doubleday, Garden City, 1979.

Mann, Thomas, *Joseph and His Brothers*, Secker & Warburg, London, 1934.

McFadden, Steven, *Profiles in Wisdom: Native Elders Speak About the Earth*, Bear & Company, Santa Fe, 1991.

McKenna, Dennis and Terence, *The Invisible Landscape*, Seabury Press, New York, 1975.

Meece, E. Alan, 'The Cycle of Cultural Change: The Uranus-Neptune Conjunction', *The Mountain Astrologer*, June/July 1991.

Michell, John, *City of Revelation*, Garnstone Press, London, 1972.

Paracelsus, *The Prophecies of Paracelsus*, Rider, London, 1974.

Puech, Henri-Charles, 'Gnosis and Time', *Man and Time*, Eranos Series, Man and Time, 1973.

Rudhyar, Dane, *Astrological Timing: The Transition to the New Age*, Harper & Row, San Francisco, 1970.

_____, *Occult Preparations for a New Age*, Quest, Wheaton, 1975.

_____, *The Sun is Also a Star: The Galactic Dimension of Astrology*, Aurora Press, New York, 1975.

_____, *The Lunation Cycle*, Shamballa, Berkeley, 1971.

_____, *The Sun is Also a Star*, Aurora, New York, 1975.

Russell, Eric, *Astrology and Prediction*, B. T. Batsford, London, 1972.

Scholem, Gershom G., *Major Trends in Jewish Mysticism*, Thames & Hudson, London, 1955.

Smyth, Piazzi, *Our Inheritance in The Great Pyramid*, Isbister, London, 1880.

Stearn, Jess, *Edgar Cayce: The Sleeping Prophet*, Bantam, New York, 1967.

Steiner, Rudolf, *Cosmic Memory*, Harper & Row, San Francisco, 1959.

———, *Earthly and Cosmic Man*, Rudolf Steiner Publishing, London, 1948.

Stephenson, James, *Prophecy on Trial*, Trans-Himalaya, Greenwich, 1983.

Stewart, R.J., *The Prophetic Vision of Merlin*, Arkana, London, 1986.

Strachan, Gordon, *Christ and the Cosmos*, Labarum, Dunbar, 1985.

Taylor, Gordon Rattray, *The Doomsday Book*, Thames & Hudson, London, 1970.

Temple, Robert K.G., *Conversations With Eternity*, Rider, London, 1984.

Thomas, Keith, *Religion and the Decline of Magic*, Penguin, London, 1973.

Toth, Max, *Pyramid Prophecies*, Destiny Books, Rochester, 1988.

West, John Anthony, *Serpent in the Sky*, Harper & Row, New York, 1979.

Woldben, A., *After Nostradamus*, (trans. Gavin Gibbons), Granada, St. Albans, 1977.

Index